THE DAYS OF RONDO

Evelyn Edwards when she was seven years old

EVELYN FAIRBANKS

THE DAYS OF RONDO

MINNESOTA HISTORICAL SOCIETY PRESS • ST. PAUL

Minnesota Historical Society Press
St. Paul 55101

Manufactured in the United States of America
10 9 8 7 6 5 4 3 2

♾ The paper used in this publication meets the minimum requirements of the American National Standard for Information Sciences—Permanence for Printed Library Materials, ANSI Z39.48–1984.

Library of Congress Cataloging-in-Publication Data

Fairbanks, Evelyn, 1928–
    The days of Rondo / by Evelyn Fairbanks.
        p.   cm.
    ISBN 0–87351–255–3 (alk. paper). — ISBN 0–87351–256–1
(pbk. : alk. paper)
    1. Fairbanks, Evelyn, 1928– —Childhood and youth. 2. Afro-Americans—Minnesota—Saint Paul—Biography. 3. Afro-Americans—Minnesota—Saint Paul—Social life and customs. 4. Rondo (Saint Paul, Minn.)—Biography. 5. Rondo (Saint Paul, Minn.)—Social life and customs. 6. Saint Paul (Minn.)—Biography. 7. Saint Paul (Minn.)—Social life and customs. I. Title.
F614.S4F19 1990
977.6'58105'092—dc20
[B]   90–35352
                                                                                      CIP

Picture Credits

The map on p. 4 is used by courtesy of McGill-Jensen Inc., St. Paul. Photographs on the following pages are taken from the collection of the Minnesota Historical Society, with the name of the photographer or other source information given in parentheses: p. 18 (*St. Paul Dispatch-Pioneer Press*), 41 and 53 (*St. Paul Daily News*), 81, 96, 97 (John Banks), 136 (*St. Paul Dispatch-Pioneer Press*), 139, 141, 144, 151 (C. P. Gibson), 152, 156 (from *The 1946 "M"* [St. Paul: Mechanic Arts High School, 1946]), 167 (*St. Paul Dispatch-Pioneer Press*), 174, 182. All other photographs are from the author's collection.

*This book is dedicated
to the people in these stories,
with deep gratitude
for the physical and spiritual nourishment
they gave to me.*

Contents

Preface

This book is a collection of stories remembered from my youth. It is important for me to tell these stories because I want others to know some of the people, events and places that made up my neighborhood. It is important for you to read these stories because no one else has told them, at least not from the spot where I was standing.

I grew up in the Rondo district of St. Paul, Minnesota. Our neighborhood was named for the street that ran east and west through it. It included the neighboring parallel streets to the north and south and ran approximately one and one-half miles.

The stories begin in 1928, the year of my birth, and continue through the Great Depression, World War II, and into the illusion of world peace and prosperity. They end in the mid-1950s, when I was a young woman.

In some ways, this is a series of personal stories, because I tell about my family, my friends on my block, and my schools. But, in a truer sense, it is the story of the times my generation witnessed in Minnesota history.

Although I had a complicated family structure, it was not unique for the times. As you read, you will come to know the samenesses of our lives as well as the differences.

Most books I've read seem to include an acknowledgment to the same two people: the typist and the editor. Until now, I didn't know how accurate the author was in saying, "I couldn't have written the book without them."

My friend, Toni Marino, typed the pages over and over and over again, always keeping a keen eye for errors and contradictions and telling me when what I had written did not make sense. But most of all, through all the delays and rewrites, Toni never doubted that the book would be published some day. My editor, Ann Regan, began working with me when I had completed twelve pages and became my friend at about chapter 6. She found the time, interest, and patience to question, suggest, subtract, think about, and harass until those first twelve pages of sentimental mutterings became a publishable manuscript.

Thank you, Toni and Ann.

A special note to those of you who lived these years with me. Forgive me if my recollections differ from yours. Or, for that matter, differ from the facts. These stories come from my memory, with all of the embellishments and deletions memories are capable of making over a long period of time. If you recognize where I have changed a name here and there, you will also know why.

Now, let's live and relive the days of Rondo.

1

Daddy

I don't remember what George Edwards looked like. I do know that he was small; but then again, maybe he wasn't. He may have just seemed small because Mama was so large. I've tried to bring his face back, but it won't come. I have a photograph of him, but that doesn't help—I only know what the photograph looks like. Did his teeth show when he smiled? Did he close his eyes when he laughed? Did he swing his arms when he walked? How did he cross his legs when he sat? All I remember about Daddy is his presence, and that presence was perfect.

We lived about two miles west of downtown St. Paul in the lower half of a duplex at 532 St. Anthony Avenue, in the Rondo district, one of St. Paul's "colored neighborhoods." "Colored neighborhood" in the 1930s meant integrated neighborhood. Not only did we have white neighbors, but there were also the white women who dated or married colored men. This seemed to me such a natural occurrence that I was almost a grown woman before I realized that Sister Tiffin, a member of Mama's church, was white.

Mama slept in the front bedroom, the middle bedroom was kept vacant for visiting Sisters and Brothers from Mama's church, and Daddy slept in the small back bedroom, just off the kitchen. We didn't have a living room; or rather, we didn't have living room furniture. The central room was our dining room, with its heavy oak table and chairs.

1

Daddy

George Edwards in front of the house at 320 St. Anthony Avenue where the family lived until 1932

I went to bed every night in Mama's bed. From the time
I could walk, Mama later told me, I made the dark journey
sometime during the night through the dining room and
kitchen to the little back bedroom. I don't remember the
trips, but I do remember waking up in Daddy's bed. I woke
up to the sounds of Daddy. He would either be making a
fire in our wood-burning cookstove, running water in the
bathroom, or filling the coffeepot from the kitchen tap.
When he got the fire going and the coffee on, he'd come
back to bed for our morning talk.

It seemed to me that we talked about everything, but
now that I think back, I know we really only talked about
my life. I could tell Daddy all the things that I kept secret
from Mama. Like about the time Donald Callender and I
lay down on one of the pews in the back of the church
whispering quietly so his sister, Danetta, couldn't find us.
Of course, she started crying, and pretty soon we heard Reverend Callender calling Donald. Well, that was the end of
that, but I sure was mad at Danetta and I told Daddy so.
He thought it was funny. He must have thought a lot of
things were funny, 'cause he laughed a lot. Except when he
said, "Ba'," — I was nicknamed for Mama's sister Alice, who
was known as Babe — "Ba', your Daddy sure loves you." I'd
always frown and say, "I *know* that, Daddy." I acted as if
it made me angry, but a warmth filled me every time he
said it. And it still does, just thinking about it.

After a little while, we got up and Daddy went off to
work at the commissary of the Great Northern Railway
Company, where he was a janitor. When he came home
from work, Daddy and I still talked a lot, but Mama was
there, too.

This routine went on every day until one evening in
January 1935 when I was six. Mama and I finished setting
the table for supper and sat at the kitchen table looking out
of the window for Daddy, because it was dark already. Daddy always got home before dark, even in the wintertime.

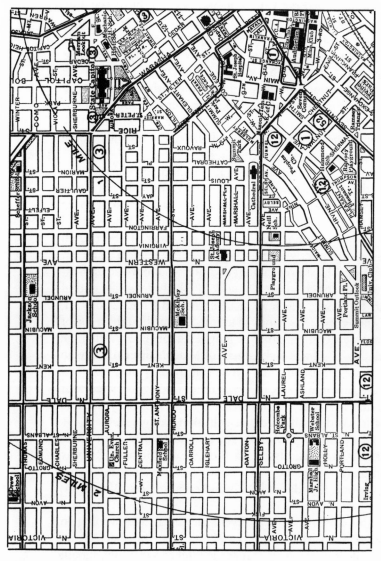

Part of a 1931 map of St. Paul, showing Rondo Avenue running east and west in the center

"Wonder what's keeping Mr. Edwards?" Mama said, more to the window than to me. (Mama always called him Mr. Edwards.) I started to worry then, not because Daddy wasn't home, but because Mama was worried.

We heard a sound on the front porch, and both of us turned that way, but then she said, "That's not your Daddy, your Daddy always comes in the back door. Must be somebody going upstairs. They sure are noisy."

Someone knocked on the door, real loud, and Mama said to me, "Ba', go tell those folks they knocking on the wrong door." Mama kept looking out the window for Daddy and I ran through the house, out into the hall. It seemed as if the entire porch was full of people, but the street light was in back of them and I couldn't tell who they were. When I opened the door I recognized Mr. Kaelble, our insurance man, with two other men. Mr. Kaelble and one man had their arms around the man in the middle. They started to follow me down the hall with me backing up in front of them. And when they got in the house, I saw the man they were holding up was Daddy.

Mr. Kaelble was talking and I was screaming for Mama. Then Mama was there asking questions. Mama told me to get out of the way and they took Daddy to his room and put him to bed. The other man went to the store to call the doctor.

While we were waiting for the doctor to come, Mr. Kaelble told us how he had found Daddy staggering and falling on the corner of Mackubin and Rondo, with a group of people standing around making fun of him because they thought he was drunk. Mr. Kaelble told them that Daddy didn't drink and that he must be sick and asked someone to help him get Daddy home. Mama kept getting up and going into Daddy's room and coming out again. I didn't say anything because I was scared, and pretty soon Mr. Kaelble stopped talking too. We just sat there and waited for the doctor.

Pretty soon Mama got up and went to the stove, felt the pot, and put more wood on the fire.

"Ba', you'd better eat your supper now."

"I'm not hungry, Mama."

Mama came over and picked up my plate from the table, took it to the stove, put my food on it, and brought it back.

"You've got to eat. I don't want you and Mr. Edwards both sick around here." She sat my plate down, then picked up the plate in front of Mr. Kaelble, Daddy's plate, and started to the stove with it.

Mr. Kaelble said, "Don't fix me anything, Miz Edwards, I'll eat when I get home."

Mama kept on fixing the plate and put it down in front of him.

"Who knows how long it's going to take that doctor to get here. You eat something."

So we ate.

After a while the doctor came and left and so did Mr. Kaelble, and Mama and I got down on our knees by Daddy's bed and prayed.

Daddy didn't go to work anymore, he just stayed in bed, and I only went in to see him when Mama was in his room, because I was afraid of him. He didn't talk like he used to, and he made funny noises that he had never made before. The doctor came every day to see him. One day the doctor said that he'd have to go to the hospital, so they took him away. I kept asking Mama why I couldn't go to the hospital with her to see Daddy, and she kept telling me children couldn't visit people in the hospital. One February afternoon Mama laid out my Sunday clothes and told me to get dressed because Daddy had been asking for me, and since he was so sick the doctors thought I should be allowed to come.

I had never been in a hospital before and at first it looked like my school. But I could tell it was a place where

people were sick because it smelled like the camphor oil
that Mama rubbed on my chest when I had a cold. The
noise was different, too. Everyone was whispering, but it
wasn't quiet. All the doors to the rooms were open, and
everybody was in bed, except for the men and women
dressed in white rushing in and out of the rooms and back
and forth in the halls. We walked a long way down the hall
with Mama telling me how sick Daddy was and how much
he wanted to see me, but that we couldn't stay too long.

I was really eager to see Daddy, because ever since the
night that Mr. Kaelble had brought him home, he hadn't
really talked to me the way he used to. Mama said that was
because the stroke had taken him out of his mind, but to
me it seemed to have taken him out of that little body lying
in his bed, too. I had saved up lots of things to tell him,
so I was walking ahead of Mama when she called quietly to
me.

"He's in this room, Ba'."

I went back to the door where Mama was and looked in
the room. There were two beds, or rather one bed and one
crib. Mama walked toward the crib and reached in and
touched him and said, "Mr. Edwards, I brought Evelyn."

"Ba'? Ba'?" That sounded like Daddy, so I went to the
bed and looked at him. He still didn't look right.

"Why are you in a crib, Daddy?"

"He's not in a crib, Ba'. They've just got the sides of the
bed up so that he won't fall out when he turns over in his
sleep."

"But he's not 'sleep now. Why don't they take them
down?"

"Ba', Ba', your Daddy sure loves you." He said it slow,
but that was the first time he had said it since he had been
sick and that meant he was getting well.

"Mama, make them take the sides down on the bed."

"Girl, why are you so worried about the sides on the
bed? Just talk to your Daddy."

"I can't talk to Daddy. I can't get in the bed."

Daddy didn't say anything else. He just lay there and breathed kind of hard. Mama said that we'd better go now, Daddy was getting tired. I reached in between the bars and poked Daddy's arm, but he didn't open his eyes again. I kept poking. "Daddy, wake up, I know you're not 'sleep." He played this game with me a lot of times. He'd pretend that he was asleep, and then after awhile he'd sit up real fast and say, "Boo!" So I kept poking. The nurse came in then and Mama told me to say good-bye to Daddy and to wait for her in the hall. Mama used that tone of voice that meant business. I said good-bye to Daddy and left the room. Pretty soon Mama came out of the room and we took the streetcar home. Mama didn't say much and neither did I.

That night Daddy died.

Since Daddy had never set foot inside Mama's church, his funeral was held at Neal's Funeral Home, which was across the alley from our house. They might as well have held the funeral in the church, because all of the members of the church attended the funeral, and Reverend Lawrence, the pastor of Mama's new church, preached the sermon. The worst part of the funeral was viewing the body. Two of the church members escorted Mama to the coffin and stood there with her while she looked at Daddy. Then two of the members walked with me to view him. When we got in front of the coffin, I turned to go back to my seat, but they held me so that I would have to look longer at the man lying there. I was terrified, because I couldn't get away. I just had to stand there until they decided to move.

After the funeral the procession went to the cemetery and Daddy's casket was put in a vault. In April, when the ground had thawed enough to allow digging a grave, we all went out to the cemetery for a graveside service. After they lowered the casket into the ground, everybody bent over and picked up some dirt from the pile that was around the grave, and Mama said, "Pick up some dirt, Ba'." I picked up some dirt and when Reverend Lawrence said, "Ashes to ashes, and dust to dust," everybody tossed their handful of dirt on top of Daddy.

On the way home in the big car, Mama looked down at me and asked, "What's that you've got in your hand?" She lifted my hand up from my lap and turned it over and said, "Ba', why have you still got that dirt in your hand?"

"I didn't want to throw dirt on Daddy."

She looked out of the window and then put her arm around me and very quietly said, "I know, Ba', I know."

Daddy was gone, but he had left me a legacy in the form of a friend. The Christmas Eve after he died, right after dark, someone knocked on our front door. As usual Mama said, "Wonder who that is?" and I gave her my standard answer: "I don't know, Mama."

Mama opened the front room door and looked down the hall to the front door, but whoever was knocking was on the front porch, at the outside door. That meant it was a stranger. Everyone who wanted to see us came into the entryway and knocked on our hall door. And everyone who was visiting the people who lived upstairs went all the way up the stairs and knocked on that door.

Mama went down the hall with me right behind her and opened that door and called through the outside door, "Who is it?"

"Is this the George Edwards residence?"

Mama frowned as she stepped into the small entryway between our hall door and the outside door. I stayed in the hall.

She opened the door. A white man stood there in a dark coat covered with large snowflakes.

"Mrs. Edwards?"

"Yes, I'm Mrs. Edwards. But my husband passed on earlier this year."

"Yes, I know. Do you have a daughter named Evelyn?"

"Who are you?"

"I was a friend of your husband. He and I worked at the Great Northern commissary together."

"Oh, my goodness! Won't you come on in. No need to stand out there in the snow and cold."

"No, my wife is waiting in the car. I just wanted to drop this off for Evelyn. Her father talked about her all the time. I know that my coming doesn't replace him, but since he's not here . . . "

"Well, tell your wife to come in too."

I had just noticed that the man was carrying a bag when he handed it to Mama and said, "No, we've really got to go. This snow is really coming down and it's a long way home from here. Merry Christmas, ma'am."

"Merry Christmas to you, sir. And God bless you."

The man turned to go and then turned back.

"Tell Evelyn Merry Christmas, too."

Mama stepped aside to reveal me standing in the hall.

"Tell her yourself. Did you say what your name is?" Without waiting for an answer she said to me, "Evelyn, this is a friend of Daddy's."

"Merry Christmas. Your Daddy spoke of you often."

And I said, "Merry Christmas."

As the man left, we walked back in the house.

"What's in the bag, Mama?"

"How do I know, Ba'?"

"Open the bag, Mama!"

"Don't get so excited." Mama set the bag down on the front room table. I could see apples on the top, those big Delicious apples Mama loved.

"These sure are some nice apples."

"What else is in the bag, Mama?"

Mama took the apples out, and then an envelope. It was sealed.

"This has got your name on it."

She handed me the envelope. I just looked at it. I didn't ever get sealed envelopes.

"Well, open it, Ba'!"

While I was opening it, Mama said, "Mmmm, look at these big pretty oranges."

"Mama, there's a dollar in the envelope. A whole dollar!"

I had never had a dollar before, either. I didn't know what to do with it. So I just held it in my hand. Mama took the oranges out and then handed me a bag of hard Christmas candy. Christmas was about the only time Mama bought candy. Now we had two bags.

Then she took a package out of the bottom of the bag. When Mama unwrapped it we saw it was a chicken. So the man became "my chicken friend."

That was the first of nine times he showed up at our door on Christmas Eve, always with a bag holding the same contents. We found that he raised chickens, that he lived in White Bear Lake, and that his name was Anderson.

During my sixteenth year he didn't come and we thought he was sick. But the next year he didn't come either. By this time, I was old enough to realize I had never properly thanked him. And so I tried to find him. I called all the Andersons in White Bear Lake, but none of them was him. Or none of them admitted to being him. And so he left my life. His going had been as sudden and unexpected as his coming. But he had extended Daddy's love nine more years.

2

Mama

Throughout her adulthood, Willie Mae Brimberry Edwards weighed at least three hundred pounds and stood a firm five feet ten inches tall. She was a warm breathing mountain of power and womanhood. To this day, womanhood and bigness are synonymous to me. Mama worked hard to fatten me up, but I've rarely weighed more than a hundred pounds, except when I was pregnant, and I stand only five feet, one and three-quarters inches.

The resonance of her voice filled the room and all its corners, whether she was speaking normally or whispering quietly to me.

Everyone was afraid of Mama except for Daddy and me, and with good reason, because Mama intended to have her way 100 percent of the time. Since Daddy and I had accepted this, our lives, while governed by Mama's wrath, were not filled with fear, for her wrath was tempered by genuine love for us.

Like most people her size, she spent a great deal of time with food, producing it, canning it, cooking it, serving it, and eating it. But the part that fascinated me the most was what she did with the food from the time she put in on her plate until she ate it. With deep concentration she mixed, seasoned, arranged, and rearranged her food. The right amount of vinegar on the greens, to the drop. The raw onions and tomato cut up with half of the greens, meat cut

Members of the Sanctified church at a picnic in Como Park, about 1934. Mama and Evelyn are seated at the far right. Others pictured are (standing, from left) Florence Wilson, Brother Hampton, Junior Briley; (seated) Sister Tiffin, Sister Briley, Sister Gude, Sister Hampton, unknown, unknown; (seated on ground) Homer Briley, Alice Lawson, Mildred Gude, Puddin' Hampton.

up with the other half. The hot-water bread torn in pieces to be used to pick up the food with her fingers. Although Mama taught me precise table manners at an early age, she rarely used silverware to eat. The food on Mama's plate looked better than any other food. Sometimes I would ask her to fix my plate like hers and she would, but it still didn't taste the same. Many times I would beg for her food. She'd always say, "Ba', it's the same food you've got on your plate." I'd always answer, "But it's not fixed the same." Then she'd shake her head and smile and I could hear that soft rolling laugh deep inside her chest as she extended her fingers and thumb and picked up food from her plate and put it on mine. Whether it was biscuits and syrup or crackling bread or navy beans, the food from Mama's plate was the best food in the world.

Mama was a strict disciplinarian and believed that if you spared the rod, you spoiled the child. She had no intention of spoiling this "grave responsibility that God has given me." My behind and legs knew the sting of the freshly cut switches Mama used for her rod all summer. I can't recall what she used in the wintertime, but since I also can't recall going without spankings for half of the year, I suppose she laid in a supply in the fall.

Mama's discipline, however, was balanced by the sense of security she placed around me. I may not have been afraid of Mama, but I had acquired the usual number of childhood fears about other things. Mama made it very clear that she intended for me to walk through the world as fearlessly as she did. (The only person I ever heard of who walked through the world as fearlessly as Mama was Harriet Tubman.) She taught me that all fear could be overcome. For example, after Daddy died she made me responsible for looking after the furnace at night.

Banking the furnace for the night was the easy part. The light at the top of the stairs lit the bottom of the stairs, but I had to walk through the dark to turn on the light by the furnace, which left the storage space behind it and the other half of the basement, containing the furnace for the upstairs tenants, in deep shadows that stimulated the imagination more than total darkness. To bank the fire, I shook the ashes down from the grate into the bottom, put any clinkers in a bucket by the furnace, and opened the damper and the furnace door. Then I went back to the coal bin, unlocked the door, and carried the coal shovelful by shovelful from the bin to the furnace, carefully picking up any I dropped on the way. Then I covered the coal with ashes, closed the furnace door and the damper, relocked the coal bin, turned off the lights, and the job was done.

Some nights this was all there was to it. Mama went

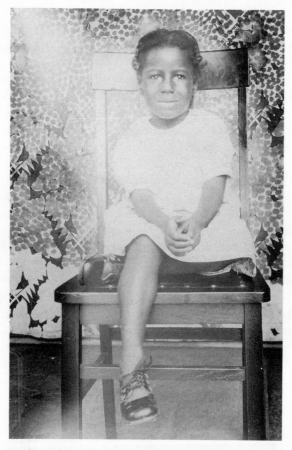

Evelyn, about four years old, in the house at 532 St. Anthony Avenue

down in the morning and brought the fire back to life. But sometimes I didn't do it right, and in the middle of the night Mama would wake me up and say, "Ba', I think the fire's going out. It's getting cold in here." That meant that I had to get up out of my warm, safe bed, put on my one-piece red snow-suit, go down to the basement, and fix the fire.

I was always scared to go down to the basement in the middle of the night, but I knew that nothing I said would save me from the trip. The sooner I got up, the sooner I'd be back in bed.

I usually found that I had left the damper open, which had caused the fire to burn too fast. I had to repeat all of the steps that I had done earlier. It was worse when we were almost out of coal because then the coal was way in the back of the bin, where the light didn't reach. Not a glow went into the darkness. I would stand there looking into the blackness, feeling with my shovel for the pile of coal. When my shovel didn't find it, I had to go into the darkness, step by step, pushing the shovel ahead of me on the floor, until finally it struck the small pile in one of the corners. But each time I went into the darkness, I did so with a bit more bravery, until I had all of the coal I needed.

It wasn't just the near-empty coal bin that held terror, for even when there was plenty of coal, the big empty space behind the furnace and on the other side of the basement seemed to be full of things that made tiny noises when the rest of the house was so quiet. I kept dropping coal on the floor that I had to pick up, all the while being watched by those things in the shadows. I wanted to cry, but that would have made too much noise, and I wouldn't hear the things; and besides, Mama would get mad if I cried.

And then, one night, the worst thing that could have happened, happened. I was almost through putting the coal in the furnace, just two more shovelfuls and the ashes, when the light by the bottom of the stairs went out. I was standing by the furnace under the light, and all around me was dark — the space in back of the furnace, the other side of the basement, and the space by the stairs where the coal bin was — and I still had to get more coal. That night I did cry. I didn't care if I couldn't hear anything, I cried *loud*. I screamed and cried until I heard that wonderful angry voice.

"Ba', what's the matter with you?"

By that time she was at the top of the stairs and saw what was the matter with me. She came down the stairs, slow and heavy.

"Girl, I thought something had happened to you. And here you are crying just 'cause the light went out. Hurry on and get through. I'll stand here and wait for you."

Mama was fussin' at me, of course, but I didn't care as long as she stayed in the basement with me.

Naturally, from then on I was afraid that the light would go out again, but it never did. Mama didn't stop me from being afraid, but she had trained me to overcome that fear. I would remember the nights in the basement the first night I stayed alone in the woods.

Mama loved to fish and didn't miss an opportunity to go. We went several times in the fall and spring, always with Brother and Sister Tiffin because they were the only people we knew who liked to fish and had a car. Most of the time we went to Buffalo, a small town west of the Twin Cities, but sometimes we fished on the Mississippi River near South St. Paul where the packinghouses were. I didn't ever see the packinghouses, but that's what they said was smelling so bad when the wind shifted.

I don't remember much more about the fishing trips, but I do remember clearly my sense of shame on the day after one, when I took the note to school. The note simply explained that I had not been present the day before because my mother had taken me fishing. If these trips had been planned, with the school's permission given before we went, I would not have been embarrassed. This was not the case. Mama went fishing any time the spirit moved her to go, and the spirit moved her every time Brother Tiffin offered to take her.

The teachers never objected, perhaps because early in my educational career they had seen my mother's wrath. When I started kindergarten at McKinley elementary

McKinley elementary school on Carroll Avenue, pictured in 1949

school, Miss Tobias sent a note home to my mother saying that I showed exceptional natural talent for the dance and that I should be given lessons. Mama didn't say anything when she read the note, but the next morning she walked me to school.

All the other kids remained at a respectful distance as we walked a half block down the alley, turned, and walked another half block to the corner of Mackubin and Rondo. The kids had to stop there to wait for the police boys to hold up their flags. You didn't have to stop when you were with a parent (and after all, there were no cars coming in 1933). So we walked across Rondo with kids on all four corners looking at us. Mama had taught me *never* to walk with my head down, so I had to look at them. There was every expression imaginable on those faces, but now and then I would see a look of sympathy.

As we entered the playground, the children stepped aside to make a path for us. Adults never changed their pace or direction when they walked through a group of children and you could always tell the bad boys in the group because they would dart out boldly in front of the adult. Boldly, but with a clear escape route.

"Where's your room?" The voice held the anger, but I was so relieved that it wasn't for me that I ran ahead of her to lead the way through the side door and down the basement stairs to Kindergarten B room.

Here the memory fades, except for Mama with her hands on her hips and the words like "Devil," "Christian," and "dance." I don't remember Miss Tobias saying anything at all, but I do remember sitting and watching from then on while the other kids danced.

Mama's ability to stand toe to toe with anyone and everything in this world was based on her absolute knowledge that God was all-wise and all-powerful and that He would use that wisdom and power to guide and protect her and her loved ones. I heard her speak these words hundreds of times. She was always saying, "God can do anything."

To prove her point, she told me about the miracles recorded in the Bible: the parting of the Red Sea, Jonah's experience in the belly of the whale, King David's triumph over Goliath, the Flood and His mercy toward Noah and his family, and on into the New Testament and the miracles that He performed through Jesus Christ. She told me about the miracles that had happened to people we knew, people who had been born in destitution and had been lifted to lofty positions as doctors and preachers, people who had been given up to die by physicians, but who had recovered after the Saints in Mama's church had stormed Heaven with prayers on their behalf. When she talked about God's miracles, she always included my coming to her and Mr. Edwards as one. It was important to Mama that I share in her belief in prayer.

One day when she was sitting in her rocking chair and I was hovering around—even though she half-heartedly kept telling me to go someplace and play—I got my foot

under one of the back rockers. I must have made a terrible
noise, because Mama jumped up, looked at the blood on
my foot, picked me up, and carried me to the bathroom.
Mama usually didn't move that fast. She sat on the toilet
seat with me in her lap and cleaned up my foot, all the time
fussing about how she had told me to get away from her in
the first place.

My big toenail was crushed and soon it was gone. The
pain was minor in comparison to the fact that my toenail
was gone. I don't know why that toenail was so important
to me, but it was. I mourned about it for days. Mama kept
saying it would grow back, but I didn't believe her. How
can a toenail grow back? "You have to pray, Ba'. God can
do anything."

"I don't know how to pray for a toenail."

"I'll pray with you."

Every day, Mama and I knelt down beside her bed and
prayed. I had heard Mama pray in church and at the table
before we ate a meal, but I had never heard her pray so
hard. She begged God to replace my toenail, not only because I wanted my toenail, but because it would create in
me a belief in prayer. Little by little I began to understand
that God had to be listening to Mama, 'cause she was praying so hard. I began to pray hard too, even though I still
wasn't quite convinced. And, sure enough, one day when
Mama was changing the white rag that she tied around my
foot, there was a little bit of toenail starting to grow. Mama
and I immediately got down on our knees and thanked
God for this miracle. The real miracle was that I prayed
harder than Mama, because now *I* believed in the power of
prayer.

Mama was big and loud, demanding and controlling,
unswervingly passionate in her love for God, Daddy, and
me, loyal to her friends, giving to sinners with hopes of saving their souls, and satisfied with life. Mama.

3

Orphans Are Made by Social Workers

I have introduced you to George and Willie Mae Edwards the way that I first met them, as Daddy and Mama. But they were not my birth parents. I pieced the story together from things Mama told me before she died and from what I learned when I went to visit Eva Mae, my birth mother, in Omaha in 1960 before she died.

Eva Mae was fifteen when she rented a room from Mr. and Mrs. Edwards. In 1928, Eva Mae Riddle was the youngest member of a small clannish family who were prominent in their Southern Baptist church in Omaha. Their prominence was based on three things: their entrepreneurship, their generous contributions to their church, and the "high yellow" coloring of their skin. This last attribute earned them the reputation of "marrying the black out of the family."

Marrying the black out of the family was not uncommon at the turn of the century. It had nothing to do with wanting to be white; rather, it was done to increase opportunities for the children. Light-skinned people were treated better and got better jobs than dark-skinned people. Blacks who did not indulge in this practice, however, often scorned those who did.

When the family discovered that Eva Mae was not only

21

Margaret Walker Riddle of Omaha,
Evelyn's maternal grandmother

pregnant, but that her child had been fathered by a dark-skinned man, she was sent away from home in disgrace. Marriage was not even to be considered.

She had a cousin working in a packinghouse in St. Paul who knew that the Edwards had an extra room. Before the open occupancy laws were passed in the 1960s, blacks who came to St. Paul could not stay in the city's hotels or boardinghouses, but rather sought housing in the black community. The Pullman porters, dining car waiters, and

*Evelyn in the yard of the house where Eva Mae worked as a maid,
about 1931*

redcaps knew of every empty room available in the city for
blacks to rent.

When I was born, all agreed that my needs would be
better served by living with a middle-aged couple who had
been unable to have a child than by a fifteen-year-old girl
who obviously was not settled yet. All agreed except the
Ramsey County Welfare Department.

When Daddy and Mama applied for adoption papers,
they were refused because of their ages—forty-five and
forty-four. (The average life-span was considerably shorter
then.) The welfare department did, however, grant Daddy
and Mama permission to keep me, and I was legally allowed
to use their name even though I was to remain under the
department's jurisdiction as a ward of the state until my
eighteenth birthday.

Sometime after my second birthday the social worker
assigned to our family decided that I should be removed
from the household and placed in an orphanage, where I

*Eva Mae and her husband, Joe Jefferson, pictured
here in Omaha in the 1960s*

would be more visible to young couples looking for a child
to adopt. Before anything could be done, I was taken away.

Mama and Daddy got in touch with Eva Mae, but that
didn't help much, because she had to prove she was a fit
mother before she could have custody of me. It took her the
better part of a year to do that. Finally, the county was satisfied when Eva Mae took a job as a live-in maid in a household where she could keep me with her, bringing me to the
Edwardses on her day off.

This arrangement may have satisfied the county, but it
didn't satisfy seventeen-year-old Eva Mae. It satisfied Mama
and Daddy even less. And when Mama was dissatisfied,
changes were about to take place.

According to Eva Mae, it took Mama about a year to get
me back. But like everything else Mama worked at, she suc-

ceeded. Except for regular visits by public health nurses, we were pretty much left alone.

Mama told me at an early age that I was not her natural-born child, and that this meant that I was a chosen child, "Not just an accident, like so many children who are with their natural parents." This was an opinion that I shared freely with my peers when I was losing an argument with them. It also had a positive effect on my childhood.

The situation was not an unusual one in our community, where many people like Mama and Daddy took care of "abandoned" children. I knew quite a few chosen children. Some were "abandoned" to a friend or relative by their natural parents during those depression years when there wasn't enough chicken in the pot to feed all of the family. Some were "abandoned" by parents who lived in the South to relatives who lived in the North where life was more generous. Like myself, some were "abandoned" to families who didn't have children by young girls who got in trouble; and, of course, the high death rate produced its share of orphans, who were raised by Big Mama (usually the maternal grandmother). Many of these orphans were nurtured and wanted by people who could never have passed the test for adoptive parents. Although most of the children in the neighborhood were raised by both natural parents, those of us who were chosen children were raised with pride and dignity.

4

God

I've always known about God. As far back as I can remember, God has been a part of my life, because God was the most important part of Mama's life. At first God was in Reverend Nelson's Sanctified church downtown, and then he moved to Reverend Callender's church on Central, and then he was at Reverend Lawrence's church on Chatsworth and Rondo, and that's where he remained until Mama died when I was eight.

Daddy didn't go to church, but Mama and I went all the time. On Wednesdays and Fridays there were prayer meetings and people gave testimony as to how God had uplifted them and changed their lives for the better. It was clear to me as a child that everyone in our church was happy, and even now as I look back (with what I assume is more sophistication) I don't remember anyone telling of hardships without adding, "But, thank God, I've still got my health and strength (or my job, or my family, or my right mind)." It seemed that whatever God took away, "in His goodness and mercy," He always left the most important thing behind.

We always had church all day on Sunday. First there was Sunday school, where we learned stories about people in the Bible, especially Jesus. We memorized verses in the Bible. That came in handy at the dinner table every evening, because everyone had to say a Bible verse by heart except

Mama, who got to make up her own prayer. Even Daddy said a Bible verse. When we had company and the Bible verses, sometimes entire passages, got too long, Daddy would always say the shortest one in the Bible, "Jesus wept." I would snicker and Mama would give Daddy and me one of her warning glances. And in Sunday school we learned the songs that we sang sometimes for the grown-ups in church service. At least, the rest of the Sunday school got to sing sometimes. I got to sing almost every Sunday, because I was "Our Little Soloist" in Reverend Lawrence's church.

In the Sanctified church, the grooming of the church Soloist starts at a very early age. During my youth there were four active Soloists at one time. The Senior Soloist was a man or woman who grew up in the church (usually with a few years' absence to serve the Devil) and who, at one time, had a beautiful voice. But the Senior Soloist's voice could no longer reach the high, or the low, notes. Out of respect for advanced years and loyalty to the church, the Senior Soloist remained in that position until death.

It was extremely easy to get the back of your mother's hand across your face if you started to laugh at a missed note.

The Soloist was a person between thirty and forty years of age who usually read music, sometimes directed the choir, and remained in this position until she or he "gradu-ated" to Senior Soloist. If the Soloist was a woman, she was also the person most likely to run off with the preacher.

The Junior Soloist category had the most turnover. These were young people in their late teens and early twen-ties who had been groomed, coached, and praised since they were the Little Soloist. Their voices and showmanship were nearly professional. Unfortunately, they were also in the prime years to serve the Devil.

Little Soloists were chosen for their big voices, willing-ness to perform, and encouraging parents (commonly known as stage mothers). I met all three requirements. In fact, I was so willing to perform that in the summer months I would stand on the top of the steps by the sidewalk and sing at the top of my voice, with a depth of feeling and freedom of spirit known only to children, loved children. So I was the Little Soloist.

My mind wandered while Reverend Lawrence was preaching, but he always got my attention when he interrupted his sermon to say, "I think I feel like hearing our Little Soloist sing a song."

When that happened, my mother got a very serious look on her face as she sat up even taller than usual and did something to my dress. She either straightened the ribbon in my hair, tied my belt again, or brushed my face with her hand to wipe something away. When she was through with me, I would squeeze past her lap (it felt so good to be close to my mother) and walk up the aisle while Reverend Lawrence quoted the verse about "Suffer little children to come unto me" or "Lest we become as children."

It seemed that I knew all of the words to all of the songs, so anything that Sister Lawrence started to play, I would sing. My favorite was "In the Garden." I used to daydream about meeting God in the garden and we would have a lot of fun playing house together. I loved to play house, but seldom had anyone to play with. Mama didn't allow me to play with any of the children in the neighborhood because their parents were not Saved. I played only with other children at church or when the Sisters of the church were visiting us with their children.

Our activities were somewhat limited, because movies, dancing, and any game that required cards or dice were sinful and the punishment was immediate. But we were children like other children, with the same energies and curiosities. So we managed to have normal childhoods— although we learned to act like "little angels" in front of

*Children of the Sanctified church at a picnic in Como Park, about
1934: (from left) Puddin' Hampton, Alice Lawson, Junior Briley,
Evelyn, Homer Briley, Mildred Gude.*

adults, as well as how to keep ourselves entertained during
enforced solitude.

When I got through singing there were a lot of calls—
"Amen," "Work through her, Jesus," and "Thank you, Jesus." Clapping, as a sign of appreciation, was considered
worldly, but the calls gave the performer the same sense of
satisfaction. I went back to my seat somehow closer to God
and certainly closer to Mama.

As soon as church services were over, the mood began
to shift from solemn joyousness to joyous activity. It was
time for the Sunday dinner. Since eating was one of the few
things in life that was not a sin according to our church
laws, considerable attention was given to it.

The men took off their suit jackets and handed them to

their wives to be folded neatly and placed on the back of the pews. We children giggled when we saw a young single man hand his jacket to one of the young ladies. That was our clue that they were "seeing" each other and therefore should be watched very closely, especially if they thought they were alone.

The men then started to set up the tables and folding chairs in the dining area, where we had Sunday school and Young People's Willing Workers (YPWW — like Sunday school for older children).

We children stood in front of our parents for instructions. The instructions were always the same, but we knew better than to leave without them. "Don't be running up and down the sidewalk. Don't get dirty. Stay where you can hear me. Stay out of people's way."

One time I did "run up and down the sidewalk" and I fell and broke my knee. All the other children stood around and looked at me, afraid to tell, because we had all been running up and down the sidewalk. Finally Mama came out 'cause she heard me hollering. She carried me into the church so that Reverend Callender could pray over the knee. He prayed over it for a week but it only got worse. Finally, Mama took me to the doctor and we found out that something was broken. I had plenty of time to stay in bed and think about what God did to children who didn't mind their parents.

Each Sunday after the children were out of the way, the women got their picnic baskets. On top were always their best bib aprons, freshly washed, starched, and ironed. (There was always a delay to admire a new apron, made since last Sunday.) Then came the freshly laundered tablecloths. These were the second-best tablecloths. The best were kept for when the preacher came to dinner. Some of these tablecloths had holes in them, but they were boiled, bleached, and rinsed in bluing. I never saw a spot on a tablecloth for Sunday dinner.

The food was brought out of the bottom of the basket with the seriousness of a sacrifice. And for good reason. It was almost always perfectly prepared. Spotless laundry and superb cooking were two skills expected among the church women. I remember how ruthlessly Florence Wilson was teased, for several Sundays, because her candied yams were too dry.

Besides candied yams there were greens, alone or mixed—collard, turnip, mustard, and dandelion—cooked with salt pork, bacon ends, or ham, which produced the pot likker that Daddy was so crazy about. There were navy, northern, or green beans, or black-eyed peas, also cooked with salt pork, bacon ends, or ham.

There was always chicken. It was fried or smothered in gravy or baked. If the chicken was baked, there was corn-bread dressing. And there was ham and sometimes beef or pork roast. In season there was rabbit, squirrel, and fish. For dessert there were layered cakes with homemade jelly filling; fruit pies with crust that really did melt in your mouth; lemon meringue pies with peaks, valleys, and caves displaying a rainbow of browns; sweet potato pies, each made from a different recipe; and my favorite—peach cobbler. And there were jars and jars of homemade relishes made from cucumbers, tomatoes, onions, green and red peppers, beets, and watermelon rind.

The children sat at tables separate from the grown-ups. But there were at least two pairs of eyes on us at all times. None of us had to be told not to embarrass our parents. That was a mistake you made only once.

At the grown-ups' table there was constant conversation and laughter over the events of the week. Many bosses would have been surprised to hear the tales told about them at Sunday church dinner. In fact, some of them became so familiar to us they were asked about every week. "Say, Brother Brown, what was Steele up to this week?"

"That man is crazy. Do you know he thinks I believe he tried to get me a raise from the Big Boss?"

"What'd he say?"

"Come tellin' me he tried his best to convince the Big Boss that I was worth more than they was payin' me."

"Don't think he did that?" (Laughter.)

"Man, the Big Boss was out of town all last week. Not only is Steele crazy, but he thinks *I'm* crazy."

One of the reasons we children could be so quiet at our table was because the conversation was so interesting at the grown-ups' table.

From time to time the women's contest to see who could make the hottest chow-chow, a relish made with vegetables, was followed by the men's contest to see who could eat the most of the hottest.

But the main thing that stands out in my memory about Sunday church dinner was the blessing of the food.

"God, we thank you for your generous gifts of food, given on our behalf. We thank you for the talents you have given these women who prepared it. We thank you for our health so that we may enjoy your blessing. We thank you for each other. And while we are acknowledging our blessing do not think that we have forgotten those less fortunate than us. So, Heavenly Father, watch over and bless and heal those of our number who can't be with us today. Seek out and find those of our families who are lost to us today and unite them once again. And God, we know you haven't forgotten the sinners; bring them in out of the cold. We know you haven't forgotten the sick; heal them. We know you haven't forgotten the tired; give them rest."

"Amen."

"Hallelujah."

"Praise His Name."

"And God, take care of our children here in our midst. Keep their hearts clean and pure and their bodies strong so that they will be able to serve you with vigor and vitality. We ask these things in the name of Jesus. Amen."

The length and fervor of the prayer depended on who was giving it. Sometimes the prayers were so long all the food was cold by the time we ate it, but no one seemed to notice except the children.

After dinner the tables and chairs were put back and the dishes were washed. The adults were quieter. Then there was a short time when the children were free to play before YPWW started.

The very young children (the people in our church always used the formal term for kids) were tucked away in little mother-made nests in the back rows of the church. When I was old enough to read, which was the criterion for YPWW membership, I would often yearn for the wonderful Sunday evenings in my little nest.

Sunday school was a good deal like kindergarten, except that everything revolved around the Bible. YPWW was a training ground for future leaders of the church and the community. The youngsters in YPWW produced Sunday youth services, which were held a few times each year. Just as the Young Soloist was found in the Sunday school choir, young men who had talent for preaching came forward in the YPWW youth services. The study of the Bible was much more than learning verses and coloring pictures of baby Moses hidden in the rushes, as was done in Sunday school. YPWW taught religious concepts and church law. Most of the Sunday school teachers were YPWW graduates. Young people remained in YPWW until they were adults.

Immediately after YPWW, evening church service started. Actually, it didn't start, it just came to be. A few people were on their knees, silently praying, others were reading the Bible, some were talking quietly in serious tones of voice, and the rest seemed to be doing nothing, but their faces showed that their thoughts were active.

After I learned to read, I used this time to look through

Mama's Bible. I realize now that it was bound in leather. Its thickness was doubled by all of the pieces of paper in it. Mama wrote down parts of the sermon and Bible verses and words to songs and sometimes people's addresses and recipes on little pieces of paper and she kept them in her Bible.

The pages were thin and made a soft ruffling sound when she turned them. I loved to look at the colored pictures of Moses and Abraham, the birth and crucifixion of Jesus, and the beautiful Garden of Gethsemane.

The Bible was never far from Mama's hand, but on Sunday evenings I got to hold it in my lap and look through all of the pieces of paper. And when Reverend Lawrence called out the text on which he was going to base his sermon, I looked up the verse for Mama.

One by one the members of the choir took their places on the chairs set up around the altar, instead of marching in as they did for morning service. As Reverend Lawrence approached the pulpit he softly started to sing a song. Something slow, half-remembered and, therefore, half-hummed. The pianist filled in a chord here and there. Members of the congregation began to focus their attention, still relaxed, nodding their heads from time to time, with some of them looking casually in the hymn book for the song.

Near the end of the song the preacher started turning the pages of his Bible, looking for his text. The song ended, the accompanist played softly.

The preacher would continue to turn pages.

"Help him, Jesus."

"Help him, Jesus."

"Help him."

"And God said unto Moses, 'Free my people.' And God said unto Moses, '*Free* my people.' And God said unto Moses, 'Free *my* people.' And *God* said unto Moses, 'Free my people.' "

The preacher read from his text and then preached on what he had read. He read from the next section of his text and preached from what he had read, again.

Slowly, but with purpose, he built the tension. He built it like a spiral in the air; each time a little higher, and between, relaxing a little, but not as much as before. And the congregation reflected the mood. They commented on his words, their voices growing louder, and someone got the "spirit" and had to be held down and fanned.

Sister Nelson started to speak in tongues and was joined by several of the other Sisters. Sister Jenkins started to cry at about the time the piano started to play; no song in particular, chords and runs. The preacher started a deep hum in between calls of "Praise His Name," "Thank you Jesus," and "My God is real."

The tempo and fullness of the piano picked up and a tambourine joined in. Feet picked up the beat as people started singing the song. It was always a fast song and sometimes the chorus was sung over and over again with everybody dancing in the aisles. And about the time everyone was sweating and breathing hard, the piano player slowed the beat down and people went back to their seats while the preacher wiped his face with a big white handkerchief and smiled and shook his head in pleasure.

"He's waiting for you. Tonight Jesus is waiting for you. He's waiting for you to come on home."

Reverend Lawrence seemed to be looking right at each person.

The pianist had drifted into "Softly and Tenderly" and Reverend Lawrence used the words of the song for the Invitational. "Softly and tenderly, Jesus is calling. If you've already given your life to God, then come on up to thank Him."

Before you knew it almost everyone was walking up the aisle. The new members were prayed over and the old members gave support to them.

After they all came back to their seats, tired but satisfied, the collection plate was passed. The preacher talked about something then, too, but no one listened. Everybody was busy getting money out, finding the children's clothes, arranging rides home, and looking after other details. Naturally, the offering was blessed, but this was a short prayer because by now people were all but walking out of the door.

No matter who gave us a ride home, the car was always so crowded I sat on Mama's lap. This was due not only to the shortage of cars, but to the fact that most of the members of Mama's church were pretty close to Mama's size.

I went to sleep every Sunday during the ride home, a sleep that was only partly interrupted by the trip into the house and the change into my bed clothes. I would remain in this half-sleep state until I felt Mama come to bed, then I moved over to her side of the bed until I was a part of her, and I slept.

5

Macon, Georgia

I met Aunt Fleta, Aunt Good, and Aunt Good's sons Morris and Oscar in Macon, Georgia, the year after Daddy died. Mama and I had taken a vacation every year in Cleveland, Ohio, where Grandma Brimberry, Uncle Pet, and Aunt Ba' had settled. But she had never taken me to her home in Macon because I was too young to understand the segregation laws in the South. But by the time I was seven, her loneliness for home got the better of her and she sat me down one day to tell me about the differences between life in Georgia and life in Minnesota.

It happened one evening after supper. Mama and I were sitting at the dining room table, she reading her Bible and I doing my homework. I knew Mama so well that I could tell her mood had changed even though I was busy with my spelling. She had stopped reading and was looking down at the table with her head turned a little bit and a serious look on her face.

"Ba'."

"Yes, Mama?" I could say "Huh?" only with other children.

"I have to go home and see my sisters. Good and Fleta won't come up here, so I have to go down there. They're my flesh and blood and I have to go see 'bout them. And I miss Macon."

"Macon, Georgia?"

"Of course, Macon, Georgia. What other Macon you know about?"

Mama never went anywhere without me, so I knew I'd have to go too. The fear took over my body and my mind, too, 'cause I looked at Mama and thought, "I don't want to go to Macon."

I must have said it out loud, 'cause Mama, frowning, asked, "What do you mean, you don't want to go to Macon?"

I had never told Mama that I didn't want to do anything, and only my great fear of the South would have caused me to voice the thought.

"I mean, I'm scared, Mama."

"Scared of what, child?"

"Scared of the things you told me 'bout."

"Things like what?"

Mama usually didn't spend a lot of time asking questions. She usually just said what was to be and that was that. This evening was different, though, and I knew she really did want to know what had scared me so much.

"You know, Mama."

"Ba', stop talking like a fool and tell what you're scared of!"

All the stories I had heard on the front porch, at Sunday dinner, under the quilting frame, all came back at once.

"Mama, I'm scared of slavery. I don't want to be a slave like, like Grandma."

"Ba', that was my grandma that was a slave, not your grandma. The slaves were set free when your grandma was a baby, so she doesn't even remember being a slave."

"But when we were in Cleveland, she told a lot of stories about slavery."

"She was just telling stories that had been told to her. There's no slavery in this country any more. You don't have to be scared of that."

"What about lynching? You were talking about lynching just the other day!"

"You don't have to worry about that. They don't lynch
women and children."

I didn't care if they didn't lynch women and children.
I didn't want to see a lynching.

"What about tarred and feathered? I heard Brother
Jackson say a whole family was tarred and feathered."

"You know as well as I do that Brother Jackson exagger-
ates every story he tells."

"But you've always said that you left the South because
of the conditions and all of the people at church say they
left because of the conditions. And everybody's always talking about slavery and lynching and tarring and feathering
and beatings, too. You told me the police beat up the
people."

The fear now had me babbling. I knew what slavery and
lynching and tarring and feathering were, but I didn't
know what "conditions" meant, and since no one told me,
I knew that it was worse than the other things. The scenes
that whirled through my head now slowed down and went
across my mind in detail, the same detail used by the
storytellers.

Mama stopped looking at me and looked up to the ceil-
ing. And then, as she lowered her head, she closed her eyes
and I knew she was praying.

When Mama was praying I didn't talk. I just sat there
and thought about the South, especially Macon, Georgia.
After a while Mama opened her eyes and looked at me
again.

"Ba', don't you remember anything good I told you
about Macon and Waycross?"

I didn't then, but I said "Yes'm," anyway.

"Don't you remember me telling you about . . ."

For a long time she talked to me gently about her home
and our family, and she ended with some Brer Rabbit sto-

ries her father had told her. And when I felt safe again, she told me about the conditions she and Daddy had left behind.

"In the South, whites and our people don't socialize together the way they do here in the North."

"What do you mean 'socialize'?"

"It means they don't do anything together. They don't drink out of the same water fountain the way you do in school. They don't go to the same bathroom the way you do in school. In fact, they don't even go to the same schools. But that part's all right because we've got better schoolteachers than the white schools. The white schools got better books and better buildings, but we've got better schoolteachers."

That must have been true, 'cause Mama had only gone to the fourth grade and she was the smartest person in the world.

"And in the South, colored folks sit in the back of the bus instead of anywhere there's a seat. In fact, when we go to Macon"—the decision had been made—"after we pass the Mason and the Dixon Line, we'll get off our car and get in a car with only colored folks in it."

"What's the Mason and the Dixon Line?"

"That's the line that separates the North from the South."

"You mean somebody drew a line on the ground all around the world?"

"They might as well have."

Mama got up and started putting the house together for the night.

In bed that night, I got real close to Mama and wondered why I had been scared. Nothing was ever going to happen to Mama, and nothing was ever going to happen to me as long as I was with Mama.

So right after the term was over, in June, we packed our clothes for a two-week vacation—plus a large trunk full of

Great Northern Railway train in the yard of the St. Paul Union Depot, 1931

clothes that Mama had gotten from the Sisters of the church for the poor people in the South. (I was full grown before I realized that there were well-educated, wealthy black people living in the South.) But I think that the main reason Mama took the trunk was that it gave her plenty of room to bring back sugarcane, raw peanuts, and paper-shelled pecans for all of her southern friends in Minnesota.

Since Daddy had worked for the Great Northern Railway, we still got free passes on all railroads even after he died. Colored people didn't eat in the diner on the train, so we took a picnic basket full of food with us. The trip for me was four wonderful days of riding on the train and eating picnic foods. We changed trains twice, once in Chicago and once when we got to the Mason-Dixon Line. The first part of the trip was quiet and I had to practice my best manners. But as soon as we boarded the colored car the atmosphere changed. There was singing and dancing and card playing and storytelling. Somebody played the guitar while somebody else slapped the sides of his legs in rhythm to the songs, and everybody was having a good time.

I knew that Mama didn't believe in all of the things that the people were doing, but she was so happy to be getting close to home that she didn't say anything. In fact, sometimes they sang a religious song and Mama sang along with them. I don't remember all of the details about the trip to Macon, but I do remember being happy and I remember Mama being happier than she had been since Daddy died.

Unfortunately, Mama lost the return pass on the train so we had to spend the entire summer in Macon before it could be replaced. Most of the time we lived with Aunt Good and her oldest son Morris, who was twenty-two. Her other son, Oscar, was twenty, and was living down the road "with a woman twice his age," which was the subject of many evening conversations when the two sisters sat on the porch cooling themselves with funeral-parlor fans.

The house had neither running water nor electricity. Laundry and sometimes cooking were done in a manner totally different from what I was used to. On washday Aunt Good pumped water from a well that was shared by several houses. She filled a big black iron pot that stood on legs in the backyard and built a fire under it. Then she put the first load of clothes (white, of course) in the pot, along with shavings of homemade soap. Aunt Good stirred the clothes from time to time while the water boiled. My job that summer was to find wood for the fire to go along with the kindling they had to buy. Sometimes I even got to put wood on the fire.

After the clothes had boiled a while, Aunt Good raised them out of the water with the stick. And when they were clean enough, she lifted them into the first rinse water. I was always fascinated by the muscles moving around like snakes under her wet dark skin when she wrung out the clothes and put them in the basket.

This was repeated until all the clothes were washed and

hung to dry. The Georgia sun dried them almost as fast as they were hung up. (If it rained, washday was postponed.) By late afternoon the clothes were washed, dried, and folded in the basket ready to be ironed the next day.

The ironing was done with flatirons heated on top of the wood-burning stove in the kitchen. The heat was so intense that Aunt Good had to wipe the sweat off her face constantly to keep it from dropping on the clothes she was ironing. It was just as hot when she was cooking, but then she could leave the kitchen.

Mama both enjoyed and took pride in her cooking ability and her skills as a laundress. But she did all of the other chores of housekeeping as if they were penance. She avoided them completely as a house guest.

"No two women can run a house at the same time," she told Aunt Good, "so I'm going to let you do it in your fashion. I'll just sit here out of your way."

Sometimes the sisters cooked outside — not on barbecue grills like those at Como Park in St. Paul, but in a big frying pan on legs that was called a spider. Anything that could be cooked on a stove could be cooked in a spider, but the best thing that was cooked in it was smothered chicken. Smothered chicken and gravy cooked in a spider with rice and biscuits, served with homemade peach preserves, is as good as eatin' ever gets.

This entire house and its functioning seemed strange to me. In Minnesota, we washed indoors and we had an electric iron. After Daddy died we bought a combination wood-burning and gas range and only used the wood-burning half for cooking in the wintertime.

Aunt Good's house was a typical three-room shotgun house.

"Why do they call this a shotgun house?"

Everybody laughed.

Morris, always the first to speak, said, "That's simple, Ba'. If you stand in the front door with a shotgun and pull the trigger, the bullet would go straight through the house and out the back door."

I was to learn years later, after I had heard this explanation dozens of times, that the long houses built by the Caribbean slaves and later the slaves in the United States were designed to resemble their homes in Africa, and the Yoruban word for house, meaning "place," sounded like "shotgun." But at the time I didn't know that, and I laughed, too, because Aunt Good's house was straight, one room after the other. The first room was Aunt Good's bedroom, then there was the living room with Morris's cot serving as a couch during the day, and after that was the kitchen. But the best part of the house, for me, was under the front porch. It was a perfect place to play because if I was very quiet Mama and Aunt Good would forget I was there and talk about all the things they did when they were young. Mama hadn't always been a Sister in the Sanctified church.

Mama was the eldest of the five children and Aunt Good (pronounced "Aint Good," of course) was the youngest. Although her given name was Arke, she was called Good as a young child by her mother because she never caused Grandma any trouble and had an easy-going disposition. The other children in the family, especially Mama, forced life to either bend or get out of their way. So it was probably a relief for Grandma to raise a child who apparently accepted life as it came. Like so many youngest children, Aunt Good had that air of innocence about her. And even though the nickname lasted throughout her lifetime, I came to understand that it wasn't because she was so good, but rather because of her nondefiant approach to life.

Like all of the girls in the family, she was tall and stately. She didn't have Mama's impressive weight, but she made up for that with her queenly secretive attitude. I've never known anyone outside of the family to address her by her first name. It was always, "Nice mornin', Miz Keaton,"

"Send Evelyn on over, Miz Keaton, and I'll send you some of my bell peppers." Everyone seemed to like her. Yet because of her standoffishness, she didn't command the loyalty of friends as the other sisters did.

Aunt Fleta, the tall skinny one of Mama's sisters, made my stay in Macon exciting. When she was born, it was as if someone had placed her in the middle of a huge carnival and told her to have a good time. According to her sisters and brother she had been that way since childhood and she stayed that way as long as she lived.

Aunt Fleta had married a man who took pride in his wife's playfulness, and he encouraged her by buying her life's little pleasures, like pretty dresses, jewelry, and a record player. Even the house he bought her was built and furnished much more like a child's playhouse than a home where serious living took place.

Her house (and it was *hers,* not *theirs*) had running water and electricity. It even had a flush toilet on the back porch. The property also included a large truck garden, where Aunt Fleta taught me to love growing things.

Aunt Fleta moved from row to row (she didn't walk; she just moved) talking to the plants, encouraging some ("You're looking better today. I knew you weren't going to die on me," or "See, I've brought the spray gun. We'll get those ol' bugs!"), scolding others ("Stand up straight! You're always standing there with your head down. What've you got to be ashamed of?"), and always touching the plants as she passed.

One day in the watermelon patch, she pulled back some leaves and said, "Ba', I'm going to give you that watermelon."

"That ain't no watermelon. That's a cucumber."

"No, Ba'. That's a watermelon. And I can tell by looking at it that it's the best watermelon in this patch."

I wasn't impressed much.

"Why is it so little?"

" 'Cause it's a baby melon. But if you take care of it, keep the bugs off the leaves, make sure it has water when it doesn't rain, and talk to it, we'll have us some good watermelon before the summer's out."

From then on that watermelon was my responsibility.

When we visited Aunt Fleta, the first thing I'd do was to go straight to my watermelon. If there were bugs or worms on the mother plant, I'd take them off and kill them with the heel of my shoe the way Aunt Fleta had taught me. And if the ground was powdery, I'd take the water bucket out and water it. And I'd pet it like you would a dog or cat and I'd talk to it, telling it what I'd been doing. And I'd tell it how proud I was of it for growing so fast and for being so pretty.

And then at last it was big enough. But every time I wanted to pick it, Aunt Fleta would thump it with her long finger and say, "It's not ready yet. It doesn't sound right."

"What's it supposed to sound like?"

"Listen. It sounds solid. Now when it sounds hollow, it's ready."

I never did hear a difference in the sound, but one day Aunt Fleta said, "It's ready."

I was so excited. I took the vine off and Aunt Fleta lifted it into my arms and I started to run to the house.

"Slow down. That melon's heavy, you know."

Of course I didn't stop running, and it was heavy, so it slipped out of my arms and landed on the ground, busted. I started to cry.

Aunt Fleta knelt down beside the watermelon and started to pick up the larger pieces and said to me, "You get the little pieces. Don't cry now, we were going to cut it when we got to the house anyhow."

I still remember how good my watermelon tasted.

Gardening wasn't Aunt Fleta's only skill. In fact, everything that she did, she did well, because she only did what she loved to do. One of the things Aunt Fleta loved to do best was dance, and even though Mama scolded her for it, she still danced. She put a record on the wind-up record player, and if it was a fast song her long arms and legs would be all over the room, her elbows and knees jutting in and out and up and down, her head jerking back and forth on her long neck, and her fingers snapping to the beat. If it was a slow song, there didn't seem to be any joints in her body, just one long smooth muscle, like a fish swimming strong but smooth, moving, just moving. Mama would shake her head in scorn. But I saw that look of love in Mama's eyes and so did Aunt Fleta.

Near the end of the summer it was decided I should be taken downtown and Morris was elected to take me. We had to walk because they were afraid I'd sit down in the front seats of the bus. Even though it was a long walk I enjoyed it, because on the way there Morris pointed out people's houses, different places family members had worked and, in between, warned me to stay close to him and not drink water out of the fountains I would see downtown.

There was a river between where we stayed and downtown. And as we approached the bridge, I pulled away from Morris's hand and ran to look at the water. It was nothing like the Mississippi, our river. It was like melted caramel. A whole river full of melted caramel!

Soon after the trip downtown, our ticket was replaced and Mama and I took the train back to Minnesota. All the way back Mama talked about how much her friends were going to enjoy the food she was bringing back in the trunk. We started our journey home in the segregated car and there wasn't much time for thinking. Most of the people on the car going South were southerners going home to visit, but most of the people on the car going North were going North for the first time. There wasn't as much singing and laughing, but it was still a happy atmosphere because the people riding that train were so full of hope for what they would find up North. Mama and I talked to a lot of them, answering many questions about jobs and houses and schools for their children. I felt very important because I was asked so many questions by both the children and the adults, and since I loved to talk, Mama had to tell me to shut up several times before we reached the Mason-Dixon Line.

When we got on the regular car, things were quieter and I spent most of the time looking out of the window and thinking about the South. The only time I saw white people all summer was the day that Morris and I went downtown. Everyone was colored. The grocer, all the delivery men, all the neighbors, even the schoolteachers, Morris said.

None of the streets in the neighborhood was paved and nobody had a basement. The grown-ups talked with the same southern accent that Mama and her friends had, and I was surprised that the children talked that way, too. There were cows and chickens along with the hunting dogs in people's yards. I had seen cotton growing and been shown how to pick it and ate peanuts right out of the ground, and I pretended that I liked them because everybody else did. Because everything was done so differently, I even enjoyed the few chores that I had. Mama complained about the endless heat, but I liked it. But what I thought about most was the conditions.

"Mama, remember those conditions that you told me about?"

Mama was looking off into space with her mind somewhere else, as she used to say.

"Mama?"

"What'd you say, Ba'?"

"I was asking about those conditions you told me about."

"I was just sitting here thinking about that. Lord, how I miss being home. I sure wish the conditions were better."

"Mama, I didn't see any conditions."

"I know, Ba', we kept you away from the conditions. If we had stayed there longer, you would have seen them. You couldn't help but see them, because they're there."

I still wasn't convinced. "I love Macon, Mama."

"I love Macon, too."

"Can we go live in Macon?"

"No."

"Why can't we go live in Macon if we both of us love it?"

"Because of the conditions."

6

Aunt Good

Sometime during that summer of 1936, Mama persuaded Aunt Good to come North to live with us. That meant Aunt Good had to persuade Morris and Oscar to leave their jobs at the Bibb Cotton Mill 1 in East Macon where they had worked "forever." And since they were both popular, they also had to be talked into leaving their friends. But Mama's stories about the North had been so full of promise for social freedom and wealth (after all, didn't we have electricity, indoor plumbing, *and* central heating?), not to mention the beautiful young women from all over the country who would be happy to accept their company, that Aunt Good had to push only a little. A few months after we came home, the three of them moved to Minnesota. They left behind everything they had except for a few new clothes that were perfect for Macon, Georgia, but not for Minnesota, a trunk full of items that they couldn't or wouldn't sell, and the usual promises to write often and visit soon.

Life didn't change much for me the first six months Aunt Good, Morris, and Oscar were here in Minnesota. Mama and I continued our regular church schedule. Aunt Good visited our church a few times, but soon found it too confining. After a few weeks she began to attend Mount Olivet Baptist, a Southern Baptist church that had not been built any higher than the basement, but swayed the entire block on Sunday morning with its "ol' one hundreds."

The Old Hundredth is known to many Christians as William Kethe's version of the one hundredth Psalm. But for black Southern Baptists, ol' one hundreds were songs of thanksgiving like the doxology, or "Praise God from Whom All Blessings Flow." They sang these songs of thanksgiving in call and response, a form brought by blacks from Africa, rather than as the hymns they were written to be. The style made it easier for slaves, who were forbidden to learn to read, to learn a new language, new religious beliefs, and new songs.

The caller said the words in a rapid sing-song manner and the congregation slowly sang the response. At least it started out that way. As the song progressed, the words took on a deeper meaning and that meaning was applied to the lives of the singers and the sorrow and the joy of their lives somehow sang out through the words. Sometimes the words were repeated again and again and sometimes another song was made a part of it and the song would take on a beat that was later to be called Gospel. The Old One Hundred hymn of thanksgiving became a joyous Negro spiritual.

Mama and I visited Mount Olivet Baptist Church a few times to get Aunt Good settled in there. The jewelry and makeup that the women wore, however, were too reminiscent of street women for Mama's conservative taste, even though she did enjoy the music.

Aunt Good never did get settled in there. A community church was much too social for Aunt Good, and soon after the need to pacify Mama was gone, she exchanged Mount Olivet for "Wings over Jordan" on the radio every Sunday morning.

I'm sure she must have noticed the difference in the weather of the North, but she never mentioned it. She accepted the weather the same way she accepted everything else in life. Only the snow, the beautiful snow, brought any remark from her. She never seemed to lose her awe of it. She looked out of the window and moved her head slowly in amazement and said, "It's like a Christmas card. It's just like a Christmas card." Other than that, Aunt Good kept her feelings to herself. The two sisters talked, of course, but the joy of reunion that had been there when we had visited Georgia was gone. We all lived in harmony that winter and spring, but I suspect that it was because no one challenged Mama's way of doing things.

On the Fourth of July, Mama did something that she had never done before except when I went to school. She allowed me out of her sight and the range of her voice. Morris asked and she granted permission for him to take me to the beach with some of his friends. We took the streetcar to Lake Phalen and I was introduced to a world that I didn't know existed. When I was out with Mama and her friends, I had fun, but only within limits of good manners. When I was at the beach with Morris, I could run as fast as I could, and I found out that I could run faster than almost anyone. The big voice that I had used at Mama's church to sing could be used to call people a block away. I could roll in the sand and get it in my hair and shoes. I could go in the water, even though I couldn't swim, and I could laugh as loud as I wanted to, and I didn't have to remember a Bible verse when we had lunch. When I came home that night, I thought that I would remember that day forever, and I have. Because twenty-four hours later, Mama was dead.

On July 5, 1937, Mama got up the same as any other day. I started the conversation where I had left off the night before about the fun I had had at the beach. All of us were talking about it, mainly because it was so unlike Mama to let me go with anyone, especially someone she considered a sinner. Even Mama seemed to enjoy the stories we told.

The day was otherwise average. Toward evening, after supper, Mama started working on half of a watermelon,

The beach at Lake Phalen, about 1935

which was also normal. She finally stuck her fork into it and said, "I think I'll give that a little rest. I'm getting full. Come on, Ba', let's go sit on the porch for a few minutes, give my dinner a chance to get out of the way for the rest of that watermelon." She complained about being too full, which was not unusual. Mama always ate until she was too full. Before long Mama said, "I'm going in the bathroom. Ba', tell Good to fix me a glass of soda water and you bring it in the bathroom. My stomach sure is feeling bloated."

Because Mama had indigestion so often, when she asked for baking soda it was like asking for the final course in a meal.

Aunt Good fixed the soda water, I walked in the bathroom with the glass, and then the day wasn't normal anymore. Mama sat there looking at me and she had death rattles. I had never heard death rattles before, but I had heard so many stories about them that I knew immediately what they were. I was scared. I started hollering wildly, "Mama's got death rattles! Mama's got death rattles!"

Aunt Good and Morris came running into the bathroom much more concerned about what was happening to me than what was happening to Mama. They soon realized that it was Mama and not me who was in trouble. Mama was trying to say something and they told me to shut up so that they could hear what she was saying.

She said, "Reverend Lawrence."

Morris took charge. "Go get Reverend Lawrence, Evelyn. Mama, help me get Aunt Willie to her bed."

I ran the half block to the corner, across the street to Jim's Bar, then across the other street to the preacher's house, stopping to tell the people standing outside the bar that Mama had death rattles. Reverend Lawrence said he was coming right away, so I ran back home screaming the same message. When I got back home, Mama was in bed, with Morris and Aunt Good bent over her, trying to hear what she was saying.

The terror I felt is beyond my ability to capture in words. Not only did I know that *I* was completely helpless, but here was *Mama,* the source of my everything, in bed struggling with all of her power to *talk.* All of her energy, her massive energy, was used, and finally used up, just to push the words around the rattles, but they never came. All I could say was, "Reverend Lawrence is on his way."

When he came, he looked at Mama from the door and said, "Evelyn, go call the doctor. You can use the phone at my house." I didn't move. I didn't know how to call the doctor. I didn't know how to call anybody. I just stood there, thinking about crying.

Morris didn't have to look at me. He knew why I was standing there. "Ba', tell any of the men standing around the corner up there by Jim's to call the doctor for you. Just give them your address, they'll call Dr. Crump for you." I went back to the corner with my new message. But the urgency didn't seem the same. Someone took my address and said they'd call the doctor and I walked back home. When I got there I was sent upstairs to the neighbors to go to bed.

Early the next morning, I was summoned downstairs. I walked down the back stairs and the kitchen door was open. Aunt Good and the boys were sitting at the kitchen table, which was set for breakfast. I just stood in the door and looked at them. Mama wasn't there. Aunt Good finally said, "Ba', your Mama died last night." No one said anything else.

The first feeling I had was nakedness. Who would protect me from the world now? Certainly not Aunt Good and her two sons who were looking at me, waiting for me to cry. Which I did, and Aunt Good said, "Come here, honey. Don't cry." She put her arms around me and they were stiff and hard, and she didn't have Mama's large, warm, wonderful bosom, and she didn't smell like Mama, and I felt a loneliness and fear deep inside my body that has never quite left.

After the funeral, which was like Daddy's except it was in the church, life took on a routine, meal after meal. Soon the three people who had to me been shadows behind Mama became real. At least Morris and Oscar became real. Aunt Good was a mystery to us all.

As far as we know there had not been a man in Aunt Good's life since her husband died, "when Bro (Oscar) was just a babe in my arms." You could tell, when she said this, that her mind was someplace else. And then she would add what I came to know as the second part of that sentence. "He told me never to put another man over my children, and I never did. No, sir, I never did."

She talked a lot about the dancing she did when she was young, and she and Morris did the two-step around the house when there was a song she liked on the radio. Other than that, she just worked around the house and sat on the front porch in the evenings, visiting with neighbors or people who walked by.

When she first came to St. Paul she did day work for families who lived in Highland Park, a new development of St. Paul populated mainly by Jewish families who had recently vacated the houses in the Rondo neighborhood that we now occupied. Later she took in laundry from neighborhood bachelors and, because she was so skilled at keeping their clothes in good repair, she never had to go outside of our home to earn money again.

Every morning, as soon as she was dressed and before she cooked breakfast, she took the broom outside and swept the front porch. Since she and I slept in the front room, the sound of the broom strokes through the open window was my signal to get up. Aunt Good never let the cold and snow change her southern habit of airing out the house while she swept.

If the rhythm of her sweeping stayed the same, I could stay in bed until she came back in and shook my bed. But if she started to sweep faster, I knew that Miz Della, next door, had said, "Mornin', Miz Keaton." Aunt Good would sweep faster, not returning the greeting, and come in the house talking to herself. To keep her from venting her anger on me, I was up and in the bathroom by then. From there I could hear this morning's version of, "Why does she always run outside and try to speak to me in the morning? She knows I don't speak to no woman first thing in the morning. She's trying to make my whole day go bad."

Aunt Good really believed that speaking to a woman first thing in the morning was bad luck. So until she spoke to one of the boys, she didn't speak to me either. When the boys moved to their own homes she didn't speak to me until after ten o'clock when Mr. Parker came by. He lived next door and Aunt Good did his laundry. Since I was usually at school in the morning or, in later years, at work, I didn't realize that he visited daily, not just on the weekend.

When I first learned that Mr. Parker was a daily visitor, I thought that Aunt Good had certainly been clever to keep secret that he had been her suitor all these years. But when I found out the truth of the matter, I was really shocked.

Mr. Parker, a deacon in the Baptist church, was also the policy man. Policy was a simple game said to have started in Italy. Once or twice a day the numbers, one through twenty-six, were put into the policy wheel (large cities had more than one) and twelve were drawn out as the winning numbers of that pull. The players chose a combination of numbers (usually four) and bet that those numbers would be pulled from the wheel. The numbers pulled from the wheel were given to the policy writers, and the writers paid the winners and collected bets and numbers for the next pull.

There was also a game called numbers that was played on the same principle but with combinations of nine numbers. Many times the policy writers and numbers writers were one and the same, although they were working for two different organizations.

I mention both games because obtaining fresh daily numbers was crucial to both. Aunt Good played policy for ten cents a day and she depended on her dreams for the numbers she played. If she ran out of her own dreams, she'd ask me what I had dreamed about the night before. Then she'd say, "Hand me that dream book in the bedroom," and she'd read me what the dream meant. At the time I didn't realize that she was interested in the number of the dream (each was assigned a number combination), rather than its meaning. I never saw the evidence of extra money in our house, so, for all I know, she spent her policy winnings on Red Seal snuff.

Policy and Red Seal snuff were the only two vices that anyone knew Aunt Good had. Unless you count her vanity and secretiveness. Her vanity was not only personal — it extended to me.

"Go in the house and comb your head, girl. Don't you know that hair is a woman's crown? Wear it proudly!"

I believe now that her secretiveness was caused by a total

lack of trust in anything or anybody, as shown in her constant advice not to put all of my eggs in one basket.

When I was a young woman starting to work, she cautioned me not to take another job like the last one. "Learn how to do a lot of things so if you can't get one job, you know how to do another one."

"Don't put all your money together. Wonder if somebody steals your purse? Be able to come home and get some more."

And when I came home excited about a new young man I'd met, without looking up from the ironing board she'd say, "That's nice, Evelyn. But don't put all your eggs in one basket."

"Evelyn, you talk too much. Don't tell everybody everything you know. That's like giving people a stick to hit you over the head with."

But being vain, superstitious, and secretive did not stop her from being a survivor in a family of survivors. And although she did not have the aggressive personality of the rest of the family, Aunt Good was still not a slouch in her ability to get what she needed from life.

For example, one winter when Morris and Oscar were only working part time and we had borrowed as many buckets of coal from the neighbors as possible, Aunt Good called the coal company and asked them to send her a half ton of coal on credit.

"First of all, we don't sell half tons of coal; and second, we don't sell coal on credit," the man told her.

Even Aunt Good didn't take no that easily.

"But I've been doing business with you for years and I always paid cash before. And now I'll need a little credit until next week."

"I'm sorry, lady, we just don't sell on credit."

"Well, if I can get the money together, you say I can't even buy a half ton of coal? I've bought a half ton of coal from you before."

"Yeah, I know. But it costs too much to deliver a half ton, so we don't sell it any more."

"Mister, you sound like you don't understand what I'm saying. I'm saying we don't have any coal in the house and we won't have any money until next week. My word is my bond. You can ask anybody. I've always paid my bills. But right now we need some heat in this house."

"I'm sorry, lady, but you'll have to call back next week when you get some money. And then you have to order a full ton. Good-bye."

Aunt Good retold the conversation three or four times to me, about what she said and what the man said and how his tone of voice sounded and how she practically begged that man "for some heat for my children." When she got through repeating the story she poured herself a cup of coffee and sat down at the kitchen table to "think on it awhile." She never prayed like Mama, but she'd sit quietly with about the same expression on her face as Mama had when she prayed. If I asked her later if she had been praying, she'd say, "No, I was just thinking on something."

I was sitting in the kitchen, too, because we had the door closed to the rest of the house and the kitchen was the only warm room. Pretty soon she got up and went back to the telephone and called the coal company again and ordered a ton of coal.

When I got home from school the next day, the coal truck was backed up to the coal chute and I could hear the warm sound of coal hitting the metal ramp. Aunt Good was in the kitchen humming "Amazing Grace." But when I asked her where she got the money for the coal, she just kept on humming. After a while, the man knocked on the door with his book in his hand and told her the price of the coal.

"Mister, I don't have any money. I'll have to pay you next week."

"What?"

"I said, I don't have any money. I'll have to pay you next week."

"Did you tell that to the man when you called?"

"Yes, I sure did."

"But we don't sell coal on credit."

"That's what he told me."

The man just looked at Aunt Good, then he looked at me. I didn't say anything. I just looked back at him.

"Lady, I can't leave that coal here if you don't have any money."

"Well, I won't have any money until next week, so I guess you'll just have to take it back."

We just stood there and I guess all of us were thinking about that man bringing that whole ton of coal up from the basement, a bucket at a time. Finally, the man's face got red and he got a real mean look on his face and said, without opening his teeth, "What day next week?"

When that man left, we sure did laugh. And when Morris and Oscar came home we laughed about it again. And then when Morris told his friends about it, standing in the middle of the floor, embellishing the story, acting out the parts with voice changes, body movements, and facial expressions, it was established as a part of our family folklore.

Like so many people of unassuming demeanor, Aunt Good was competent. About 1940, as we listened to newscasts of the war in Europe, we started hearing about shortages of several items, including metal. To the women in our neighborhood this meant canned goods. Aunt Good had enjoyed the luxury of buying the few canned goods that she used since Mama died. She had rebelled against home canning when she looked at the room full of canned fruits and vegetables Mama had stored in the basement.

"Somebody's gonna have to come and get all this food. I just can't eat food cooked by a dead woman. As ornery as

Willie was, I'd be eating that food and say something she didn't like and she'd choke me to death on it."

Morris, who was of a more practical mind than his mother, said, "Mama, times are hard. We can't afford to give away a whole room full of food."

"It's better to give it away than throw it away. I'm telling you once and for all. I'm not going to eat no dead person's food!"

Once again, her superstitions overruled any kind of practical considerations. But when the government asked "the citizens of this great country" to do without things like commercial bread slicers and to can their own food in order to conserve metal, Aunt Good's patriotism answered the call.

At the end of our block, at Mackubin and St. Anthony, there was an empty lot with a high fence around it. I don't know who owned it, but when the call for victory gardens was made, it was turned over to people on the block to be divided into individual garden plots.

Most of the people on our block had come from farms and were happy to show off their skills as food producers. As a result, from the beginning of the planting season until harvesttime, competition ran rampant.

Aunt Good was not like Aunt Fleta. She didn't seem to take much joy in gardening. Fact is, she approached gardening like she approached everything else in life. She just did it. She didn't get involved with the bragging that went on, but I heard her mumble things like, "She thinks she's the only one who ever planted a seed," or "Wait until harvesttime. We'll see who's got the best crop," or "I'd sure hate to have to eat those mustard greens. They started to get tough a week ago. Why don't she pick those greens?"

Sure enough, when harvesttime came, Aunt Good didn't have to take a back seat to anyone. And during the winter months, Aunt Good, Morris, Oscar, and I enjoyed home-canned food again.

She was so unlike Mama, neither happy nor sad, neither cold nor warm, neither hateful nor loving, neither good nor bad. She was so within herself that I never knew how she felt about me. But she kept me clean, warm, well fed, and protected, and she taught me all she knew, some things that I could understand then, and some things that I didn't understand until years later. She was important to my life because she was one of the few people who gave me all she had to give. She died when I was twenty-two.

7

Morris and Oscar

If I had lived alone with Aunt Good, I'm sure that I would have spent the rest of my childhood missing the energy and love of life that Mama had shown me. But there were the boys. Up until Mama died, they had been my first cousins, but right afterwards Morris teased Oscar, "Well, little brother, seems as if you've lost your place as the baby in the family. We've got ourselves a little sister now."

"I'm still the baby brother. She's a girl." Even though Oscar was a full-grown man at the time, he wasn't about to be nudged out of his place as Morris's little brother. I had lost my spot forever as the favored only child. But I had gained that special role of kid sister to two popular men filled with youthful fun.

As with many brothers, Morris and Oscar were as different as earth and sky. Oscar had the self-contained character of his mother. His voice was soft and he had the habit of speaking to one person in the room, allowing the rest of us to eavesdrop on the conversation. Morris, on the other hand, put on a performance. He addressed himself to the room. He seemed to be looking right straight at everybody at the same time, and every word, every pause, was a part of the story. As a child, I would rather have Morris tell me about a movie than go to see it. He was a master storyteller.

Though they were different, they were very close to each other, with Oscar living under the protection of his older

Morris and Oscar Keaton in Macon, Georgia, about 1932. The brothers were then seventeen and fifteen years old.

brother since birth. Even school didn't separate them. When Morris started going to school every day, Oscar went into mourning—crying, refusing to eat, talk, or play until Morris returned home in the afternoon. Aunt Good became so concerned that she talked to the teacher about it. Since it was a small community school, the teacher was free to make decisions that would be impossible today. She suggested that Oscar go to school with Morris and sit in the back of the room while Morris attended his lessons. Aunt

Good and the teacher thought that Oscar would soon tire of this and would ask to be left at home.

They were wrong. Oscar, with his quiet manner, sat there all day playing with a piece of paper and crayon, or a small toy, or just listening. Sometimes he took a nap. He joined the other students for lunch and recess, where some of them would tease him about being a baby. But Oscar didn't care. He just kept going to school every day with Morris. Finally, the teacher told Aunt Good, "Mrs. Keaton, as long as Oscar's there, I'm going to start teaching him, too. Maybe then he'll get tired of school and want to stay at home." Aunt Good agreed.

Again, they were wrong. Oscar was a little slow, but he kept up with the class and they remained in the same grade until they both left school to work in the Bibb Cotton Mill after the tenth year.

Even with their differences in personality, they had spent all of their lives together until Oscar had left home in Macon to live with "that woman." Now they were back living and working together.

When they first came to Minnesota, they did some day labor, then they both worked at a car wash for awhile. Later they went to work for the railroads. Morris didn't work for the "road" very long, but Oscar eventually retired from there.

After Mama died, everything changed. While my early years were full of church and quilting bees and laughter around the dinner table, my later childhood overflowed with honky-tonk music and fancy women and laughter around the card table. Even the house changed. I still had my daybed in the front room with the big featherbed that Aunt Good now used instead of Mama. The big round oak dining room table replaced the smaller kitchen table, and a living room set was bought for the old dining room. The combination wood and gas stove was replaced by a smaller gas range, and we got a telephone. Oscar had the back bed-

room that used to be Daddy's, and Morris and his girlfriend, Isabelle, used the middle bedroom that had always
been saved for the visiting Sisters and Brothers of Mama's
church. The wind-up gramophone was still in the corner of
the new living room, but now it played blues, jigs, and reels
instead of Mama's church songs. The dark, flowered wall-
paper was replaced with lighter, happier themes, and Mama's Bible was stored in the sideboard.

The forbidden deck of cards now became a part of the
household furnishings. Both of my brothers enjoyed a
friendly game of chance and saw no reason why I shouldn't,
too. Oscar's favorite sporting game was tonk. It's a reason-
ably mild game, a bit like gin rummy, with a beginning
ante, and Oscar taught me to play using buttons. The goal
is to diminish a playing hand by spreading, hitting, or
reducing the value of the cards in your hand by exchanging
them for lower cards drawn from the deck. Tonk requires
high observation skills but doesn't have the pizzazz of Morris's favorite game—stud poker.

Morris felt it took too long to learn to play if your motivation was low. He knew that playing with real money
heightened the senses and strengthened the desire to win.
I guess he knew what he was talking about, because it only
took me three allowances to learn the rules of the game.
And it took me only another four allowances to understand
that there was more to the game of poker than rules. I had
to consider possibilities of bluffing, make educated guesses
as to my opponent's hole card and rapid judgments about
my opponent's betting patterns, and figure the chances of
filling an inside straight based on cards that were showing,
how many people were playing, and how far down in the
deck we were.

Morris left me pretty well equipped when I started playing poker with the kids in the neighborhood, even though
they introduced new versions of the game. But I still don't
play a decent game of tonk.

Though I called my cousins my brothers after Mama died, in operation they became my two fathers. The twelve and fourteen years of difference in our ages meant that they were grown men, while I was still a child. In the mid-1930s, and especially in my culture, age difference was significant. It meant I was expected not to "talk back." And when I did, the words "shut up" brought instant silence. I was not expected to "roll my eyes" at them. And when I did, the command to "stop rolling your eyes at me, girl" brought a quick, respectful, downcast expression to my face. Even when I left the room after a disagreement of some kind I learned to slam the door quietly. It was understood that I was not to raise my voice in anger at my older brothers any more than I would have at Mama or Daddy or Aunt Good.

Aunt Good was now the senior member of the immediate family and was honored in that position by all of us. However, it was the boys who were the heads of the household. Morris, being the eldest, made all the major decisions. When he wasn't around, Oscar took over. Oscar was more lenient than Morris, so I always tried to catch Oscar alone to ask permission to go somewhere, or for extra money. Morris always said that there was "no such thing as 'extra' money."

For example, sometimes I would get up in the morning and remember that I needed money for something in school that day. Both of them were still sleeping. When I woke Oscar, who loved to sleep, he mumbled, without opening his eyes, "What do you want?"

I said quietly, so as not to bring him too close to wakefulness, "I need a quarter for a special tablet today."

This time, he barely opened his mouth. "So what are you waking me up for? Look up there on the dresser and get on out of here so I can sleep." Then, drifting cautiously out of sleep, he'd ask, "What time is it anyway?" I'd tell him, he'd turn over, and I would tiptoe out of the room.

If I asked Morris, which I did only if Oscar didn't have

enough, I had to rethink the urgency of the request. To begin with, when I opened the door Morris was looking right
at me, as if he'd been lying there waiting for me to come
in all morning.

"Morris?"

He never said anything, just kept looking at me.

"Morris?"

"Girl, you know I hear you, what do you want?"

"Morris, I have to have a special tablet for art class today. The teacher bought them so they would all be alike.
But we have to buy them from her today at the latest."

"When did you find out about these special tablets?"

"She told us about them last week."

"Then why did you wait until this morning to bring it
up?"

"I forgot."

"It must not be very important to you if you forgot."

"It's important. I just forgot."

"Well, maybe it is important and you thought it would
be easier to get money from me when I was half asleep like
you do Oscar."

By now I wished I had gone on to school without the
money. But I couldn't think of any way to get out of the
room. So I kept pushing forward.

"It's only a quarter."

He finally sat up in bed and said, "Hand me my pants."
And while he was getting the money from his pants he continued the lecture about taking care of the things that were
important to me and being straightforward about the
things I needed to have. It seemed as if he preached an entire sermon between the time he reached his hand in his
pocket and the time he handed me the quarter.

Throughout my childhood Morris was the most severe
taskmaster, but he was also the most giving of himself. Oscar helped to support me with his salary and he never mis-
treated me in any way. But Morris took the time to teach

me about the street and the people I would find there and
how to handle myself as a lady. We went to the movies together, had snowball fights, and talked a lot, and he shared
his women with me.

When I went to the show with Oscar, I had to sit on the
other side of Oscar's girlfriend. But when I went with Morris and his girlfriends, I got to sit between them. And how
I loved Morris's girlfriends. They all seemed so pretty to me
and they smelled so good. They wore all of the latest
fashions and knew all of the latest dance steps and slang.
And they paid so much attention to me. Sometimes they
would go away and stay several days and I was afraid that
they were never coming back. When I asked Morris where
they were, he said that they had gone to some small town
to work as dancers. He always seemed to know they were
coming back and they did. When they came back, life was
so much fun. Suddenly there was a lot of money and Aunt
Good would put on her clean apron and go to the store and
buy a lot of groceries.

One time I got to take a hundred-dollar bill to the store
to buy something. I was so proud that Morris had trusted
me with it, I showed it to everyone I met on the way to the
White Front Grocery Store.

"Where did you get that much money, girl?"

"Morris gave it to me. I'm going to the store."

"That's a lot of money for you to be flashing around."

"That's not so much money."

"What do you mean, 'That's not so much money'?
That's three months' salary."

I saw someone else coming so I skipped off to meet her
and show her my hundred-dollar bill. But I hollered over
my shoulder, "Money's not important."

Morris had taught me that money was not the most important thing in the world in one painful lesson. One
Saturday I ran into the house to ask his permission to go to
the show with Barbara Ann Williams.

"Have you got any money?"

"No, but Barbara Ann's mother will pay my way."

"Why's Barbara Ann's mother going to pay your way?"

" 'Cause Barbara Ann needs someone to go to the show with her, and I don't have any money. The show starts in a little while."

"I didn't ask you when the show started. We're still talking about Barbara Ann's mother paying your way. Do you want to go to the show with Barbara Ann?"

"Sure."

"Let's put it another way. If you had your own money, would you go to the show with Barbara Ann? For example, if Blanche Everson would come over and she had her show fare and you had your show fare and she wanted you to go to the show with her, would you still go with Barbara Ann?"

"Morris, you know that Blanche is my best friend. Of course I wouldn't go with Barbara Ann."

"Oh, I see." Morris always said "Oh, I see" when he had me trapped.

"Maybe I'd go with Barbara Ann," I said quickly.

"Evelyn, you and I both know that the only reason you're going to the show with Barbara Ann is because she's got enough money to pay your way. Girl, let me tell you something that I want you to remember all of your life. Don't let money make your decisions for you. Make your own decisions."

"I am making my own decisions."

"No, you're not. Barbara Ann's money is making the decision for you to go to the show with her. You just said that if you had your own money, you'd go with Blanche."

"But Blanche isn't going to the show. So I want to go with Barbara Ann. Morris, it's almost time to go and Barbara Ann's waiting for me."

"Well, if she's waiting for you, you'd better go tell her you're not going because you don't have any money."

I stood there, but I knew nothing would change Morris's mind. So, after a little while I went outside and told Barbara Ann that my mean brother wouldn't let me go. She asked why, and I just said, " 'Cause he's mean." Now Barbara Ann couldn't go to the show, either.

I went back in the house, because Morris's tone of voice had said that he wasn't through talking to me. I went in the room where Morris was and sat down.

"Ba', I don't want to be mean to you, but I don't want you to go through your life hating everything around you 'cause you get so excited about that almighty dollar. I know some women that work on a job for years just because it pays a little more money than a job they'd like to do. They marry a man they can't stand to have around just 'cause he's got a steady job and brings home a little paycheck every week. Then they have a houseful of kids by this man and they can't stand the kids either 'cause they look just like their daddy."

I laughed at that. Morris always said something funny when he was talking serious to me.

"And that ain't all. They associate with people they don't like at all just because those people have money to spend on them. That's what I call letting money make your decisions for you. They spend their whole life letting money use them instead of them using money. And it's not just women that do that. My buddy, Richard, married that old, ugly woman last year just because her mama had died and left her a little piece of change. Now he's ashamed to take her to the grocery store."

We both laughed. Morris liked that story so he made a long series of jokes about his friend's ugly, old wife.

I had forgotten all about going to the movies and Barbara Ann. But then Morris brought the subject back.

"Now, would you be having this good of a time, if you were at the show with Barbara Ann?"

I shook my head, still laughing at Morris's jokes.

"That's all I wanted to tell you. Go on outside and play now. Just remember, don't let money make your decisions for you. You'll live a happier life if you don't."

So, as I ran to the store showing off the hundred-dollar bill, I knew that I was impressing some of the folks, but that "we" didn't think money was important.

Naturally I had favorites among Morris's women, and one of them was Isabelle. When Isabelle came back from out of town, she gave me her dirty silk stockings. "If you want to wash these, Evelyn, you can have them. I hate to wash stockings." Of course I was thrilled. Not only did I like to wash the stockings (silk feels good when it's wet), but I was the only kid my age with silk stockings. She paid me to run errands for her and polish her leather shoes. Behind Isabelle's back, Aunt Good always said she was lazy. But Aunt Good liked her, too, because she was so easy to get along with and stayed out of Aunt Good's kitchen.

Isabelle used to read to me. She loved *True Confessions* magazines and lots of times she went to bed early so she could read. She'd start getting ready for bed and call to me, "Evelyn, if you put on your pajamas and get ready for bed, I'll read to you."

So I washed my face, brushed my teeth, put on my pajamas, got the pillow from my bed, and went into her and Morris's bedroom. She was already propped up on the two pillows, ready to read a story she had found. To a thirteen-year-old, the people in the stories seemed very sophisticated. Their lives were full of adventure and told of a world that I had never seen or heard of. Isabelle's voice was soft and low and had a rhythm to it like a slow song. When I first got in the bed I always put my pillow at the foot so I could watch her while she read. Isabelle's skin was the color of coffee with three spoons of cream in it. And with her flat-surfaced face and shoulder-length pageboy hairstyle she looked much like the beautiful Japanese women I saw in the movies. But soon her face would be replaced in my mind's eye with those of the characters in the story. And it was like watching a movie as she read.

When she stopped to light a cigarette or drink water, her face came back into focus. But as soon as she started reading again, the images returned. Sometimes Morris came home before the story ended and I begged him to let me stay there until the end. So he went into the living room and talked to his mother until Isabelle finished reading. Then I went to the room I shared with Aunt Good and went to bed with the sound of Isabelle's voice, the smell of Morris's cigar, and visions of the people in the story all easing me to sleep.

I enjoyed the card games, dancing, and especially the house-rent parties. From time to time, we didn't have the money to pay the rent. Then we took what little money we had and bought groceries, liquor, and a new deck of cards. Aunt Good cooked pots of food and sold dinners, while Oscar sold drinks by the shot and Morris dealt the card game. At the end of the night we'd have the money for the rent. It seemed that almost every month, someone was giving a house-rent party, and it was always well attended.

I can't say if life was better or worse without Mama and Daddy. Aunt Good and the boys had witnessed Mama's method of discipline and felt that I had had enough beatings to last me for the rest of my life, so I was never again to feel the sting of the freshly cut switch. However, I was a willful child and every other kind of punishment had to be used to keep me from taking over the household. I guess the truth is that life was not better or worse, it was just different.

8

Perfect Days

The summer breeze came through the screen and the lace curtain and across the room and got in bed with me. For a long time that's all there was, just me and the breeze. I didn't have to look — I had seen it come in so many summer mornings in my nine years, barely moving the curtain a few seconds before it reached me. I just lay there with my eyes closed and felt it. After a while, I heard the noises. Not loud, just the noises of summer. A robin starting a melody, a jay demanding something, a squirrel teasing a cat, and one of my playmates acting as if she was having *so much fun* in order to attract someone else outside to play with her.

Inside the house there was the sound of breakfast. Breakfast sounded slightly different from other meals. Aunt Good, Morris, and Oscar were talking quietly, laughing now and again, not like laughter at the supper table, just breakfast laughter. There were more trips to the stove, and while there didn't seem to be any hurry in the movement, there was purpose. But it was the smell that finally got me out of bed. The smell of the damp earth coming in with the breeze and joining the smell of pancakes, maple syrup, bacon, and coffee convinced me that there was a better place to be than in bed.

I got up and took off the long white cotton nightgown that had been Aunt Good's (I thought it was so fancy, even

74

though I couldn't walk in it), and I put on my underclothes and the cotton dress that wasn't as stiff this morning as it had been yesterday when I had put it on fresh from the laundry. Aunt Good didn't think that anything had enough starch unless it could stand up by itself.

Since we were not considered presentable until we had washed up in the morning, I hurried through my toilet, then went to say good-bye to the boys before they left for work. I followed them out the back door and into the yard and started to walk down the alley with them, when Aunt Good came to the door and said, "Girl, get in here and eat your breakfast. Do you think I want to be in the kitchen all day?"

I came back in the house and started talking to Aunt Good even though I knew she wasn't interested in what I was saying, until finally she said, "Shut up and eat your breakfast. I've got something else to do besides serve breakfast all day." She said that almost every morning and every morning I just shut up and ate my breakfast. I didn't care this morning, anyway. There were other things I wanted to do, like playing outside.

Years earlier, Mama had made it clear to our upstairs neighbors that the yard and the porch belonged to me during the day and my family during the evening. In the corner of the front yard, near the sidewalk, was what I called my vine house. It was a thirty-six-inch wooden bench with spaced boards on three sides and the top, which someone had planted grapevines around. From spring until fall the structure was completely covered with leaves, except for the opening. Its entire floor space was no more than nine square feet and it was tall enough so that I could stand on the bench. To an adult it was probably only a seat. But to me, it was a complete world.

After breakfast, I gathered my box of paper dolls, a pair of scissors, and the Montgomery Ward catalog, peeped out of the front door to make sure there were no kids around, and quietly ran from the door to the vine house. I didn't really like to play with my paper dolls with other kids 'cause they bent the dolls' heads and arms and sometimes even tore an arm or head completely off. If I was careful not to let them see me, I would have an hour or so alone before someone came into the yard and found me.

This morning was one of those wonderful times when I found a lot of clothes in the catalog to fit the paper dolls. Sometimes clothes were hard to find because they were either the wrong size, facing the wrong way, or for the wrong sex. (In the early 1930s you couldn't put jeans, or any other pants, on girl paper dolls.) No one came to look for me, so I spent the entire morning finding clothes, cutting them out, and acting out scenes for the dolls with their new wardrobes.

Lunch was biscuits with homemade syrup, which meant we didn't have much food in the house. But that was all right with me because I loved biscuits and syrup.

After lunch I went out in the backyard for my other favorite activity, one that I didn't mind sharing — making mud pies. Even though I always made cakes, they were always called mud pies.

Making mud pies was a real art that took a lot of practice. And I practiced almost every day in the summer. I had to get the right kind of dirt, not too much sand or it would fall apart, but not too much sticky dirt either or it wouldn't come out of the jar lid that served as my baking pan. Then I added just the right amount of water. I had to be very careful not to waste water, 'cause I could only get it once from the outside faucet. If I tried to sneak some more, Aunt Good would hear it in the house and make me stop playing outside, because "Obviously you don't know how to mind, so come on in this house!"

This morning I sneaked some black dirt from the fishing-worm bed and smoothed it back over so I didn't leave a hole. Then I got some sandy dark dirt near the steps and, stirring with a Popsicle stick, poured the water in very slowly because the dirt from the worm bed was damp already. When it looked just right, I put the mixture in the jar top, making sure it was pressed down evenly all over so there wouldn't be any air holes. Then I put it in the sun to bake while I made another one. While they were both cooking, I went to the spot between the neighbor's fence and the back of the garage and dug up some light brown dirt I had found the previous year. It was exactly the right color for frosting. This part was really tricky 'cause one drop of water too much would make it runny and you couldn't make designs in it. By the time I got it nice and smooth, the pies were ready so I turned them out on my tin pan. Neither one of them broke or stuck in the jar lid. I frosted the first layer and then carefully lifted the second layer on top of it — not a crack in it. Then I frosted it, too, and put swirls on it and peaks that stood up straight. It was perfect.

After all those years of trying, I had finally made the perfect mud pie. So I ate it.

About that time Aunt Good came to the door to call me in (she still practiced "comin' in out of the heat of the day"), and she caught me eating the mud pie.

"Girl, how many times do I have to tell you to stop eating that dirt?"

I wasn't eating dirt, I was eating a mud pie.

"I keep telling you and telling you, all those dogs and cats running around through this neighborhood. You don't know what they're doing on that ground."

I knew exactly what they were doing on that ground, but they were also doing it on the dandelion greens, and we ate them all the time.

Of course all these thoughts were in my mind. I wouldn't have thought of saying them out loud. Any reply to a scolding was "sassin' back" and sassing back was always punishable.

I put my pans and bowls and Popsicle sticks away and

went in the house to wash up and settle down to something quiet. Something quiet meant sewing, reading, coloring, or any other activity that didn't require Aunt Good's attention. Actually, it was a quiet time for her, when she could slow her work pace, prepare for dinner, change into clean clothes, and not worry where I was or what I was doing.

This afternoon Morris came home early. And an afternoon of his playfulness and funny stories passed quickly into dinner. He even made washing the dishes fun, sitting at the kitchen table with his long legs spread apart and his heels touching (I always tried to sit like that and I never could), talking to me as if I was the most important person in the world.

After a while he got up and stretched, took two steps in place, and hiked his trousers up, and that was the signal to me he was going to leave for the evening. I always hated to see Morris go, but even without him, evenings were nice at my house. The older folks gathered on the front porch to talk. To keep the mosquitoes away, they made a smudge pot, taking a ten-pound chitterling (pronounced chitlin') bucket, putting rags in it, and setting the rags on fire. Then they put more rags on top, putting out the flame but keeping the fire going enough to smoke. Sometimes they fed the pot with fresh grass or weeds. I don't know which was worse — the mosquitoes or what happened to your eyes and lungs when the wind shifted too quickly for you to move out of the way.

The conversations usually started out with events of the day — who had a new baby, who had moved, and who had died — which usually reminded someone of somebody else who had died in the past, and that was the beginning of that evening's ghost stories. Everyone on the porch believed in the ability of the dead to walk the earth, so everyone got comfortable and listened to the person telling this evening's story. We children got comfortable on the stairs (only adults could use the chairs) and waited to be scared out of our minds, again.

This evening it was Aunt Good who said, "I've got to get a new front step put on. I'm seeing Willie" — that meant Mama — "entirely too much in this house." All of us knew that a person who died in a house came back to haunt it until a new bottom step was put on the house. Then the ghost couldn't recognize the house and therefore wouldn't come in. My stomach turned into a rock.

"The other night I got up to go to the bathroom and there she stood in the door to the bathroom. And I just said 'Get on outta that door, Willie, I ain't scared o' you!' and she just laughed and disappeared."

The rock in my stomach was getting bigger and harder and it was easing up toward my throat.

Aunt Good kept talking about all the times she had seen Mama in different parts of the house, but I just kept seeing her in the bathroom doorway. And the more I saw Mama filling up that bathroom door, the more I had to go to the bathroom.

Now, I knew I couldn't see Mama, or any other ghost, as some of the grown-ups could, 'cause I wasn't born with a veil over my face. People who were born with a veil over their face could see ghosts from the time they were babies. Since I hadn't ever seen one, everybody knew I couldn't. But just because I couldn't see them didn't mean they weren't there.

"So the next time you see Mr. Bailey, send him by here to put me on a new front step."

Since most people died in their homes in those days, Mr. Bailey did a thriving business putting on new front steps.

When the story was over, I was told to go into the house and go to bed. "And don't be wasting that electricity. You know where everything in the house is."

I glanced down at the new step that Mama had put

down when Daddy died, even though Daddy had died in the hospital. Mama said Daddy came back to the house anyway 'cause he was so crazy 'bout me. I didn't move off the step until Aunt Good turned and gave me that look of hers.

I went in the outside door and stood in the front hall that led to the upstairs. I looked hard down the long hall that went to our door but I didn't see Mama, so I went in. From the moment that I got into the house I kept my eyes steady on the door that led to the bathroom. I didn't see Mama there either, but I knew she was standing there and I knew she wouldn't like it if I was scared to go past her to the bathroom.

As I got close to the door I figured that if I pressed my body right next to the door frame I could get by her without touching her. I had seen Mama standing in that door so many times before she died that I knew she almost filled up the door. But there was one small sliver of space for me to slide past sideways. I did. And while I was in the bathroom, Mama left, so I walked out through the middle of the doorway and went to the bedroom. I put on my long white gown and went to bed thinking about all the paper doll clothes I had found, my perfect mud pie, and being "Mama's brave little girl."

Another day that I relive for its joy is the first time I went to the Orphans' Picnic, that same summer.

Losing your parents is a high price to pay for anything, but, like most things in life, it has its compensations. The "Orphans' Picnic" was one. For most of the first half of the century, the St. Paul Fire Department gave a picnic each year for orphans at the amusement park in Excelsior, west of Minneapolis. They took the residents of St. Joseph Orphanage, which was run by the Catholics, a Lutheran orphanage, and a third one that I don't know by name, plus those of us who had been lucky enough to be wanted by a family.

Excelsior Amusement Park, Lake Minnetonka, 1933

One day, a year after Mama died, Aunt Good told me a car would be picking me up to take me to Excelsior Amusement Park, a magic land I had only heard of, for an all-day picnic. Naturally, that news was more than I could stand by myself, so I ran out of the house and across the yard and alley to Blanche's house, where we had been playing before I was called in for lunch.

Of course Blanche wanted to go 'cause we were best friends. But when we asked her mother, her mother said no because Blanche wasn't an orphan. Blanche threw a temper tantrum the same way she did when I got to have glasses and she didn't. And finally her mother made Blanche go to her room and sent me home. The next morning, early, before the car came to pick me up, I went over to Blanche's house to tell her I wouldn't go if her mother wouldn't let her go just because she wasn't an orphan. I really felt sad about going anywhere without Blanche. And I felt especially bad because she wanted to go. When I walked in the house Blanche was eating breakfast and she was still so sad she wouldn't even look at me.

"I'll stay home with you and I'll even let you play with my paper dolls." Now that was really going some; that was the ultimate sacrifice.

"I don't want to play with your old paper dolls. I want to go on the picnic. Why do you have to be an orphan anyhow?"

"I don't know. I just am. I wish you were an orphan."

"So do I."

Mrs. Everson got upset again and hollered at Blanche.

"How can you wish your father and I were dead just so you could go on a lousy picnic?"

"I don't wish you were dead, I just want to be an orphan."

I could hear my aunt calling me then and I didn't know what to do. Mrs. Everson solved the problem by saying, "Even if you don't go to the picnic today, Evelyn, you can't play with Blanche today. I've got some work for her to do."

So, if I couldn't play with Blanche, I might as well go to the picnic. The car came as soon as I got back home, and it drove me to a corner where a lot of other kids waited to take the streetcars to the park.

Excelsior was a long way from St. Paul and sometimes the track ran right through miles and miles of woods. So it was more like a train ride than the streetcar rides I had taken downtown. To my surprise, I knew a lot of the other kids.

That ride sure was fun. It was the first time I had been on a streetcar without a lot of adults. Every time we passed a fire station, we yelled at the top of our voices,

Two, four, six, eight,
Who do we appreciate?
The Fireman! The Fireman!
Rah, rah, rah!

By the time we got to the park, I had forgotten about Blanche. The firemen had rented the entire place, and we filled it up. They gathered us to tell us the rules. We got a long strip of tickets for the rides with instructions to come back for more when they were used up. And we got another ticket for lunch that we weren't supposed to lose, although almost everybody did. We were told not to get in the boats by the lake without an adult and not to leave the park. Fortunately, that was about all, 'cause we were too excited to be still very long.

It was a day kids dream about — carnival rides, hot dogs, and freedom from adults' constant warnings. On the way home that evening we were quieter than on the ride out, except when we passed a fire station. As we neared home, I began to think about Blanche and wondered if I should tell her about all the fun we had. Maybe I shouldn't.

I went on that picnic several times and today, fifty-plus years later, whenever I pass a fire station, I think, "Two, four, six, eight, . . ."

9

The Visitors

When I was a girl, we could learn about the activities of our community without ever leaving our house. I don't think a day went by that someone didn't come to our door. The Sisters and Brothers with their families from Mama's church; friends of Aunt Good and the boys; my friends knocking shyly and asking, "Can Evelyn come out and play?" Every day someone came.

But the visitors who gave our life so much variety were the people we did business with. And while they weren't exactly friends, they were part of the neighborhood, and there was still a lot of conversation and good will between us. Except for the ragman. With the ragman there was a lot of conversation, but very little good will.

The ragman drove a horse and wagon and you could hear him a block and a half away, calling "Yeggs, yeggs." (I know now that he was saying "Rags, rags.") If we had something to sell that was small enough to carry, we took it out on the front porch and waited for him to get to our house.

As he came closer, we could hear the "dho plou dho plou — dho plou dho plou" of the horse's hooves on the soft asphalt. I don't know how often he came but when he did he stopped at almost every house, because if we didn't have something small enough to bring out, chances were that we had something in the house he had to help carry.

During the depression very little was thrown away. What little food was left went to the hunting dogs. Clothing was mended, handed down or over, taken in, let out, and then finally made into quilts. Other cloth items, like towels and sheets, also had long and varied lives. Glass jars were used for tableware or canning. Paper, wood, and cardboard were fuel. Fish scales and guts were buried to fertilize the garden. Coffee grounds were sprinkled over the fishing-worm bed and then covered with a staked-down gunny-sack. What was left was sold to the ragman.

The price was predictable. It was a rare item that brought more than ten cents, although a heated argument could raise the price by a few pennies. I don't know who enjoyed those arguments more, buyer or seller. I do know that Mama prepared her argument well in advance with the same attention a lawyer uses to prepare a case for the jury.

"Lady, this is just a piece of junk. But I'll give you a dime for it."

"A dime? Man, you must be out of your mind!"

"Look at this table, the varnish is all worn out and the legs are loose." While he said this he chipped at the varnish with his dirty fingernail and shook the table to prove his point.

"Man, this is a good table and you know it. It just needs a little glue. And there's nothing wrong with the finish on that table."

"I don't think I even want it. What am I going to do with a table in that condition?"

"I keep telling you. This table's in good condition. My dead mother gave me this table when she was alive. It sat beside her bed every night and it's given me good use for years. You know there's nothing wrong with this table. I just don't have room for it any more."

"Lady, I don't have all day to stand here arguing with you. But as long as I've spent this much time, I'll tell you what I'll do. Just to show you I've got a heart, I'm losing money, mind you, but I'll give you twelve cents for that old table."

"Humph! You don't do nothing but ride around here with that old horse and cart and steal from poor folks. But I don't have no place to put it, so I guess I'll have to let you steal it. Give me that piddling twelve cents."

Now that wasn't a bad few minutes' work, considering women were doing daywork for a dollar plus carfare and lunch. So, good will or not, he had his place in our lives.

Another regular visitor was the corsetiere, since most women were walking proof of their cooking ability. Mama had three corsets. Every afternoon, after her work was finished, she called me in to be cleaned up. For me, it meant a bath, a clean dress, and, worst of all, no more playing in the mud until the next morning. For Mama it meant bathing and putting on a fresh dress and apron smoothed over her everyday corset. The second corset was her good corset, worn for visiting and going downtown to shop and pay bills. Mama didn't have a checking account, nor did she trust money orders. She did all her business in person with cash. And then there was the Sunday corset, for church and special events like funerals.

As time and Mama's body took their toll on the everyday corset, the other two were shifted down and word was sent to the corsetiere to stop by the next time she was in the neighborhood.

I can't remember her name, but it was something fancy, which means it was probably French. Many of the Creoles who came to St. Paul had French surnames. Her clothes were not remarkable, but I do remember how she looked and smelled. Her complexion was pitted, and she brought attention to it by wearing an abundance of makeup. Her fragrance was so strong the house smelled of her long after she was gone. Mama certainly didn't approve of her, but since she had something Mama needed, a visit from the corsetiere was friendly.

The coal man and vegetable man were not greeted with preparation and expectation, but from time to time I would get instructions like, "Sweep down those basement steps. You know the coal man comes tomorrow and he may need to go in the coal bin to push back the coal."

Probably the best-informed visitor to our house was Miss Jackson, the hairdresser. In order to become a hairdresser in Minnesota, the State Board of Cosmetology required 1,500 hours of training to obtain a license. This was one of the highest requirements in the nation, and most beauticians coming from other states had to return to school to qualify for a license. But none of the 1,500 hours was devoted to working with skin of color or kinky hair. Black beauticians who moved to Minnesota had no motivation to go back to school to meet the requirements. Nor was there any reason for a young black girl to train, since she had to learn how to pull, straighten, curl, wave, and cut the hair she would be "beautifying" on friends and relations. Practicing on the white women who were the customers of the beauty school was a waste of time. I had heard of only one black woman who worked in one of the downtown shops.

This situation produced hairdressing bootleggers. They normally traveled to their customers' homes to keep their neighbors from reporting them to the authorities for some sort of illegal activity. Sometimes other people came over to our house to get their hair done at the same time, so it would be an all-day procedure, taking on the merriment of a quilting bee.

Miss Jackson was a square-built woman whose only moving parts were her arms and legs. The rest of her body was strapped in place by the bones of her corset. She moved rapidly and her presentation was businesslike. Her actions made it clear that she had come to work, not to socialize, so when she arrived our hair was already washed, neatly braided, and dry. The kitchen was spotless, with all foods covered and a chair placed by the stove. Miss Jackson set her little black bag on the floor (no one allowed anything that touched hair to be placed on the kitchen table) and took out her straightening combs, curlers, pullers, crimpers, and rags for wiping the heated irons. Then she struck the match and lit the gas burner on which she would heat the irons.

Before the natural look became acceptable (to blacks as well as to whites), getting your hair done was a lengthy process, and — if you didn't keep your head still — a painful one. I hated it, and I was always glad when I could be first, so I wouldn't have to think about it all day. Miss Jackson was fast and efficient, but she was far from gentle.

First she combed the kinks out of my hair with the large straightening comb. Then she used the hot pullers (tongs with ball ends flattened on the insides) to straighten small clumps of hair. The small heated straightening comb was used on the short hair around the edges of the hairline, sometimes producing burns. You could also be burned if the curling iron got caught in the little curls; feeling the heat, you might pull away and bring the hot iron onto your head.

But beauty is in the eye of the beholder, and we all thought we looked better after we had gone through this painful and sometimes disfiguring exercise at least twice a month. (Rain, humidity, or sweat could undo the job in less than an hour.) Someone always remarked about how *everyone* could understand why Madame C. J. Walker, who invented and marketed the lotions and straightening combs we used, was the first black millionaire in this country.

Miss Jackson worked quietly while the women busied their hands with knitting, darning, or turning the collars on their husbands' shirts. The conversation worked itself around the neighborhood about the latest doings. She didn't really participate in the gossip except to correct an occasional bit of misinformation. Every now and then I could feel her body move in back of me as she laughed, not with her face, just with her stomach.

When she had finished all of the "heads," she collected her pay while the irons were cooling on the stove, packed them away, and, with a mind full of new information, walked rapidly to the next house.

I am truly grateful for the youth of the 1960s, who saw beauty in naturalness.

There were other visitors, of course: the doctor, the street vendors selling hot tamales and household trinkets, the organ grinder (without a monkey), and the iceman. On hot summer days the iceman was special for us kids. We gathered around the back of his truck and he gave us ice chips to eat. And sometimes, when there weren't any on the floor of the truck, he chipped a piece off with his ice pick, just the right size, and that was our treat for the day.

And there were the bums, who came to the back door and asked if they could work for a meal. Mama always had something they could do. And when they finished mowing the lawn, or cleaning the basement, or fixing something that was broken, she had a plate of hot food ready for them. They sat down at the kitchen table with me and Mama (I was almost always allowed to be around if I didn't say anything), and Mama asked them about their adventures. Sometimes they were from places where Mama knew people, and they talked about prominent people like the preacher or undertaker or café owner. And sometimes they talked about places they were going later in the year to look for work, and Mama gave them names of relatives and friends to go to. When they had a particularly long talk, Mama packed a lunch and sent it along with them. Since we never had store-bought lunch food in the house, these lunches were simply leftovers from the meal: biscuits or corn bread, meat, and whatever sweets she had baked.

Every day it was someone. Then the visitors were gone. The neighborhood had changed.

I was not aware of the change when I was a child. Sure, people painted their houses, or moved to other houses, or even left town. The young women had babies and the old people died, and people went south to funerals and brought back relatives, but the neighborhood stayed the same. I mean, life in the neighborhood stayed the same. Then one day I went to high school and when I came home, it had changed.

Mothers were working in factories, stores, war plants, and a few offices. Women were driving cars and some of the young people weren't going to church at all. People were buying living room sofas that didn't have to double as beds because most of the roomers had saved enough money to send for their families and set up housekeeping for themselves. Almost everybody had a party-line telephone, so children didn't have to "Run over to Mrs. Warren's house and give her this note. You don't have to wait for an answer, so come straight back home." (Coming straight back home meant that there was time for a cookie at Mrs. Warren's house or a quick game of jump rope on the way.)

The telephone stopped those little visits for the children. A lot of other things stopped the visits for parents. People with steady jobs didn't have to hustle for themselves anymore. Labor-saving home appliances allowed mothers to take full-time jobs. People were beginning to mistrust the strangers that came to their doors. They started paying their bills by mail instead of paying the salesman who came to collect every week. There are a lot more reasons, I'm sure. The truth is, though, I miss them. I truly miss the visitors.

10

Mrs. Neal and Her Daughter Albreta

Of course, the visitors were only a small part of our community, which had a social structure as complex and as rigid as that of the larger community around us. When I was a child and young woman, the blacks in St. Paul earned their money in work that fell into four categories: entrepreneurs, professionals, "servants," and packinghouse workers. (I use the word "servant" in the broadest sense, to include railroad porters and waiters, men who worked in car washes, and people who worked in restaurant kitchens—not as cooks.)

The distinctions were not at all clear-cut. For example, a man who shined shoes in his own shoeshine parlor was considered a businessman, but if he shined shoes in a white barbershop for the tips he received, he was a shoeshine boy, a form of servant. It might be simpler to say that there were no black factory workers, office workers, retail clerks, waitresses, waiters, or health or education workers, except in black-owned enterprises.

The entrepreneurs owned a few grocery stores scattered here and there, a drugstore, a record shop, and a few bars and restaurants. The barbers, who started each day by going to the homes of wealthy white customers to shave beards and cut hair, had shops in their own homes for the neighborhood people.

In my family's immediate neighborhood there was Black's Grocery, the Majestic Drug Store (always known as Fields' drugstore for its owner), Jim's Bar, Mrs. Dandridge's restaurant, the Carobama Restaurant (named for the two southern states that produced its owners), and McCoy's Tailoring and Cleaning, where I took Morris's and Oscar's trousers and suits for a quick "sponge and press" between dry cleanings. In most cases the businesses were directly across the street from their Jewish counterparts. For a few years the shops operated side by side, but gradually the Jewish businesses followed the Jewish customers to their new homes in Highland Park. The blacks moved in to fill the houses with families and the storefronts with churches.

The businesses sometimes provided more for the neighborhood than just whatever they were selling. For example, members of the Communist party held their meetings at Mrs. Dandridge's restaurant. Not many black people were members, but a lot of people went to their meetings because the Communists helped the unlettered migrants in working with the various systems that were new to them. Getting help from government agencies was much more cumbersome than going to the Big House for assistance, as they had done in the South. People from rural areas had not had experience with unemployment insurance, loan companies, mothers' aid, county hospitals, and, later, social security.

Another business for entrepreneurs were the "good-time houses" (now called tippling houses), which were popular among my crowd, although they were subject to raids. There were several, but probably the most notorious was Good Daddy's, which continued to operate into the 1950s. His success was in no small part related to his downtown connections. No one knew exactly what those connections were, but we did know that they were effective. We had all partied at Good Daddy's, heard the phone ring, and

seen Good Daddy turn the jukebox off and announce that
we would have to leave because he was going to be raided.

We finished our drinks quickly while we located our
coats and purses. The ante money from the gambling pot
in the middle of the kitchen table was put in an empty
coffee can and placed on the shelf. Someone always said,
"Man, can you believe this? The first decent hand I've had
all night and that's when the man's coming. If it wasn't for
bad luck, I wouldn't have any luck at all." With a quick decision on where we were going, we emptied the house within five minutes, except for Good Daddy and a couple of his
friends sitting around having a drink. And that's what the
police found when they came. In about an hour the phone
rang where we were and we all went back. The jukebox was
plugged back in, the drinks were served again (on the
house), and everyone stood around the poker table to see
who would win this interrupted pot. The winner would always say, "I keep telling you people, if it's meant for you,
you'll get it," bragging about Lady Luck and fate smiling
on him, until someone would say, "Man, shut up and deal
the cards."

There were only a few black professionals, including
members of one professional baseball team. The St. Paul
community supported two medical doctors, Dr. James W.
Crump and Dr. Val Do Turner, three dentists, Dr. Albert
M. Butler, Dr. Earl S. Weber, and Dr. Charles H. Williams, and a handful of lawyers who had exchanged the
right to practice law in their home states in the South for
the social freedom of Minnesota. So they worked for the
railroad and practiced law (usually in an advisory capacity)
in their spare time.

By the time I got to high school there was one black
teacher in the St. Paul school system. But Miss James was
so light-skinned that only members of the community
knew of her black heritage.

Most of the blacks worked as employees in service-related jobs. Among the largest employers of black men were the Great Northern and Northern Pacific railroads, which hired them exclusively as waiters and porters. These jobs were considered to be excellent, with steady work and good tips. Private families also employed blacks as maids, cooks, nannies (we called them baby-sitters), and chauffeurs. Although these people worked as domestics, the positions weren't necessarily menial. A man or woman who had been in the service of a wealthy family for years wielded great power in the household, as well as in the private lives of family members.

Since some of the neighborhood people worked in personal service, blacks knew many of the wealthy and powerful families in the St. Paul area. The families who worked for the wealthy acquired the tastes of the wealthy. It was not unusual, at the home of a poor black, to have a meal using sterling silver, hand-painted china, and lead crystal, with original oils and watercolors hanging on the walls. Some of these were gifts to the employees made during times of house remodeling. And at other times, the maids would put the articles on lay-by (a dollar down, a dollar a week) until a birthday or other gift-giving holiday came along, and then "Miss Anne" would say, "Have you still got that place setting on lay-by?"

"Yes. And I haven't missed a payment. I'll be able to get it out in no time."

That was the signal that Miss Anne intended to present it as a gift to the maid.

This mirroring of life-styles by the blacks also extended to articles of clothing, leisure-time activity, and speech patterns. A servant's vocabulary and grammar often belied his or her limited formal education.

Social clubs paralleled the exclusive clubs of the rich. Political groups were as active as their white counterparts. And the worship service and songs of the two elite black churches, St. James African Methodist Episcopal Church and Pilgrim Baptist, were more comparable to the conservative white churches than to the Southern Baptist and Pentecostal churches that Mama and Aunt Good belonged to—although, I must admit, both St. James and Pilgrim sported very good gospel choirs in addition to their senior choirs.

The black class system did not operate by ranking actual jobs. Status was based on *who* you worked for rather than *what* you did, with self-employment being the highest. A maid for an old wealthy family was above a maid for a young professional family, just as a janitor for the Golden Rule was a decided step above a janitor for Woolworth's. The salaries were pretty much the same, but the gifts from the wealthy were considerably more generous. The favors included such things as vacations, large Christmas bonuses, employment for other family members, and much more consideration for the employee's personal life.

Another crucial indication of social status was address, especially for the blacks who lived in Rondo. The houses at the east end of Rondo, between downtown and Western Avenue, were called Deep Rondo (later called Corn Meal Valley) and made up the least desirable neighborhood. Between Western and Dale was the middle ground without a name. West of Dale Street to Lexington Avenue was a coveted area known as Oatmeal Hill. Also, the farther north or south of Rondo Avenue a person lived, the higher his status. Just as the banker who lived on Summit Avenue recognized but did not socialize with the mailman, the servant of the banker who lived on Rondo and Lexington recognized but did not socialize with the packinghouse worker who lived on Rondo and Farrington.

Our family lived between Kent and Mackubin, in the "middle territory," and sprinkled here and there in that middle ground was a family of high status like the Neals, who lived directly across the street from us.

The eldest member of the Neal household was the

*The intersection of Rondo Avenue and Arundel Street, 1940 —
part of the "middle territory" of the Rondo neighborhood*

widowed Mrs. Bell, who came to Minnesota as a bride with
her barber husband in 1886, the year of St. Paul's first Winter Carnival. (Members of the Neal household always spoke
of Mrs. Bell's arrival in that manner.) Also living in the
house were her daughter Eva, who insisted even as a child
that her first name be pronounced as if it were spelled Ava;
Eva's husband, Thomas Neal, who was also a barber and
had a downtown shop; their son Andrew, who seemed to
be away at school most of the time; and their daughter
Albreta. The entire family was considered high society by
the black community because of their entrepreneurship,
early migration to Minnesota, activity in political, social,
and church functions, grace of manner, and, to some ex-
tent, color of skin—or rather, lack of color.

    Mrs. Neal was very active in political and educational
"worthy Negro causes," so that many times she would have
houseguests who traveled to Minnesota to raise funds for
national causes. In 1938, Mary McLeod Bethune was a guest
of the Neal household when she was on a national fund-

Thomas and Eva Neal, who lived on St. Anthony Avenue across from Evelyn's family

raising tour for her school, Bethune Cookman College in Florida. Mrs. Neal used her connections, and all the connections of her friends, to insure that the fund-raiser was a success.

Mrs. Neal was a charter member of the Council of Negro Women. Besides doing behind-the-scenes work for voter registration, members lobbied for bills that would affect the status of blacks, both in Minnesota and throughout the country. They assumed that blacks needed the assistance of

the greater population, and the women felt that the only
way to get help was to be able to talk to powerful people
on their level and on any subject. They took advantage of
all opportunities. For example, in 1941, when First Lady
Eleanor Roosevelt came to St. Paul for a political rally, the
group, in the person of Mrs. Neal, presented her with a
bouquet of flowers. Mrs. Roosevelt sent the group, in the
name of Mrs. Neal, a thank-you note; Mrs. Neal later wrote
and asked her to use her influence on civil rights legislation.

There were quite a few of these women, active for the
betterment of their people, who produced children similar-
ly active. As Mrs. Bell had trained her daughter, so had
Mrs. Neal trained hers. And when Albreta was well on her
way to being a productive young lady, Mrs. Neal turned her
attention to me.

Their house became as familiar to me as my own, because from the time Mama died until I started to work at
the Star Laundry when I was fourteen, it was my job to help
clean that house every Saturday. For me, it was a way to
earn money. But for Eva Neal, it was an opportunity to give
me a thorough cultural education.

The summer between my third and fourth years in
school, Mrs. Neal explained the differences between a salad
fork, a dinner fork, and a dessert fork on Saturday while I
cleaned house, and Albreta taught me my multiplication
tables on weekday afternoons. This was a major undertak-
ing for the teen-aged Albreta, especially since arithmetic
was a land of mystery to me and rote memory the dullest
possible way to spend a summer afternoon. But she kept at
it and never got discouraged enough to give up. And that
year, in the fourth grade, I found myself in a position I had
never been in before or since. I was the smartest one in the
arithmetic class all year long.

Mrs. Neal was very different from the women I had
known. Although she was a prominent member of St.
James church, she didn't have the religious fervor of Mama

and the Sisters at Mama's church. Nor did she have the
knowledge of "worldly things" that Aunt Good and my
brothers' girlfriends had. She had a whole different realm
of knowledge and style. No matter what she did, it always
seemed to be the "right" thing. Her temperament was
even—I never heard her raise her voice in anger or laugh
out of control.

"Evelyn, your voice is too loud. You *must* learn to control it. Ladies don't raise their voices."

She didn't wear fancy clothes like Morris's girlfriends—
her clothes were always tailored and the correct subdued
color.

"Evelyn, don't ever wear red. Red is the color for street
women."

She had great influence over my wardrobe, too, because
before I started working in the laundry, she bought and
made, and made over, most of my clothes.

"This skirt fits all right, Mrs. Neal. I don't care if it's too
loose around the waist. I'm going to wear a sweater over it
anyhow."

"Always buy the best clothes you can afford. Alter them
so that they fit correctly. Keep them clean and repaired and
you'll always look proper."

Lots of people have said that, but with Mrs. Neal it was
a way of life, a philosophy that extended to her home. It
looked better than any I had ever been into. I know it was
relatively small, because none of the houses in the neighborhood was large. The barbershop that Mr. Neal operated
during those years in the closed-in front porch didn't stop
it from looking grand to me.

The fancy parlor contained gleaming tables and ruffled,
starched doilies and overstuffed furniture that looked as if
it was never sat in. The dining room had a large heavy table
with clawed feet that needed dusting in between the toes,
a china closet with matching dishes and silver in the top
drawer that needed cleaning and polishing several times a

year, an oriental rug on the floor that had to be taken up, put on the clothesline, and beaten twice a year, and little figurines that broke so noisily. In fact, the entire house had that proper look—including the kitchen, which never seemed to contain dirty dishes. Even the clothes that hung out on the line on washday looked already ironed.

Mrs. Neal dwelled in and presided over that house as a queen would over a kingdom. And that kingdom included me, even after I stopped working for her when I was fourteen—dating age. Early one Saturday morning she called me on the phone.

"Evelyn, when it's convenient, would you please come over here? There's something I'd like to discuss with you."

The words were not unusual. She always spoke politely. There was an edge to her voice, however, that warned me that she was unhappy with something I had done.

"Yes, ma'am. I'll be right over."

Aunt Good was in the kitchen when the phone rang.

"Who was that?"

"Mrs. Neal."

"What'd she want so early in the morning?"

"I don't know."

"Well, what'd she say?"

"She just said to come over there."

"What'd you do wrong?"

"Nothing. I didn't do nothing wrong."

Aunt Good went back to cooking, but she still said loud enough for me to hear, "You must have done something wrong. She wouldn't be calling you over there for nothing this early in the morning."

Aunt Good didn't like Mrs. Neal any better than she liked anyone else, but she respected her. Although she didn't oppose the training I was getting, she'd sometimes just grunt and look away when I told her something Mrs. Neal had said.

I got dressed, taking care that I looked neat, and ran

across the street and around the house to the back door. Mrs. Neal was in the flower garden. When she saw me she straightened up, took off her gardening gloves, and asked me if I had had breakfast.

"No, ma'am. Aunt Good's cooking now. We're going to eat in a little while."

She went into the house ahead of me and sat in her chair at the kitchen table. I took my seat across from her. She got right to the point.

"I see you had a date yesterday evening."

"Yes, ma'am. We went to the movie show. He came in the house to get me and we were back home by the time Aunt Good said I had to be back home." I tried to cover all the bases in one breath.

"I see you were back home at a decent hour. But I was wondering what was so important that the two of you had to sit on the front steps and talk about it for an hour."

"We didn't sit outside for an hour."

"It was an hour."

There was no point in my going any further with that argument. If Mrs. Neal said I had sat and talked for an hour, it was an hour.

"Well, we just hadn't finished talking. And besides, the street light was shining right on us."

"I know the street light was shining on you. That's why I saw you and that's also why everybody else saw you."

"But we weren't doing nothing but talking."

"That's not the point. The point is that when a young man brings you back home, the date is over. If the two of you have so much left to talk about, he'll ask you for another date. Now, wouldn't you like to go out with that young man again?"

"Yes, ma'am."

"Then, the next time you go out with him, at the end of the evening tell him that you had a lovely evening and

'Good night.' Ladies should not be seen loitering with men. Don't let your company be so easy to come by."

"But what if we're right in the middle of a conversation?"

"After you've dated a young man a few times, and it's early in the evening, you can ask him to come in the house and have some refreshments. But don't stretch it out too long. There's always another day."

I left Mrs. Neal's house pretty mad. What did she know about dating? I could hardly wait to get home and tell Aunt Good what she had said to me. But when I had repeated the conversation to her, mocking Mrs. Neal's proper way of speaking, Aunt Good looked at me for a moment and then said, "She's probably right. It doesn't pay to be too loose with men."

Naturally I couldn't let it rest at that. I told Morris about it when he came home from work that evening.

"Well, Evelyn, she's got a point. I know that I'm a lot more eager to go out with a girl that draws the line someplace than one that doesn't."

As always, Morris made more sense to me than anyone else. So from then on I said "Good night" when my date brought me home.

After high school, I moved away from home and the watchful eye of Mrs. Neal. As a young adult, experimenting with life, I took a certain joy in disregarding the lessons she had given me. Even now, I don't always play the part of a proper lady, but I have been deeply grateful for the ability to present myself in an appropriate manner when necessary. And ever since I finally grew old enough to recognize it, I have been deeply grateful for Mrs. Neal's love, as well.

11

Little Girls and Little Boys

In the beginning, my social life was conducted within range of adult eyes (which could see around corners), hearing (which could identify all activity by its sound), and intuition (which bordered on the psychic). This surveillance was not only used to keep us safe—our parents were also teaching us the differences between the roles we must play as little girls and little boys.

"Little girls don't fight."

"Little boys don't cry."

"Little girls are pretty, and pretty is as pretty does."

"Little boys are mannerly, and strong, and brave."

"Little girls are gracious."

"Little boys are helpful."

"Little girls wear dresses, and keep them pulled down."

"Little boys wear pants, and keep them buttoned up."

The list of differences never ended, for when we mastered the correct behavior for one age group, the ritual for the next age group began. And the rules became more complex as we got older.

"Girls don't wrestle with boys."

"Boys open doors for girls."

"Girls don't call boys on the telephone."

"When boys are visiting the home of girls, they always

hold a conversation with the parents of the girl until the parents dismiss them to pay attention to the girl."

As young as we were when this all started, it produced a mounting curiosity about the other sex. A mounting curiosity leads to dating. I began dating before I was five years old. Of course I had to depend on Mama to take me to church or to visit her friends who were parents of my current date. But we could pretty well count on our parents for their cooperation.

When I said to Reverend Callender's son, Donald, or Reverend Lawrence's son, Richard, or Sister Hampton's grandson, Puddin', "See you next Sunday," we had just made a date.

When I had made a date, I would always ask Mama if I could take my braids out and let my hair "hang." I thought I looked pretty when my hair was "hanging."

In fact, my hair was not hanging at all. Mama brushed it and tied the ribbon on top instead of underneath, where it could hold the hair down. My hair was shoulder length, thick, and bushy, and by the time I had tossed my head up and down and back and forth to show off, the ribbon was off and my head looked a great deal like a porcupine. It would be several more Sundays before Mama let my hair hang again.

We didn't really do anything different when we were dating than when we were just playing, but every act, every word, and every gesture was made to impress. Even though the roles of little boys and little girls have changed in the last fifty years, the behavior of childhood dating has remained the same.

After Mama died I practiced these roles on a larger scale, because I was allowed to play with the neighborhood boys and girls. And in addition, Aunt Good, who didn't care Bo Diddly about the Sanctified church in the first place, told me that I didn't have to go there anymore if I didn't want to. It took me only a few weeks, with the Sisters and Brothers of the church picking me up for all-day Sunday service, to see that I didn't want to. I didn't like being at church without Mama. Everyone there was kind to me, but I didn't seem to belong anymore. All of the children had someone special who cared about them, but I didn't. And it was lonesome without Mama's lap to fall asleep on.

Besides, there were my new playmates. They only stayed in church a few hours and then they were free, after family dinner, to play or go to the Sunday matinee movie. And they made jokes about the people who went to my church. They imitated people who "spoke in tongues" and "got the spirit," which caused them to cry out and jump around and fall on the floor. It didn't take many of these sessions for me to be ashamed of the church and the people who belonged to it. Since Aunt Good, Morris, and Oscar only visited churches from time to time, the choice was to be completely my own. I began to go to church with my new friends, except the Catholics, whom Mama had especially distrusted.

Finally, Mrs. Neal noticed that I was doing too much church visiting and persuaded my family to let her take me to her church, where she could watch out for me. Now, besides the children in the neighborhood, I also had new friends at St. James African Methodist Episcopal Church on Central and Dale. Every Sunday morning I received six cents — five cents for Sunday school collection and one cent for candy. I usually put one cent in the collection and spent five cents on candy during the time between Sunday school and church service when the children were allowed to "work off some of their energy outside."

After eight years of playing mainly alone, I now began to learn the games of the street. At first, the games merely reflected the life that we observed: church, school, store, doctor, and house. Then we began to play the activity games that really didn't have a goal, but were simply something to do. Giving the impression of being pretty was a big part of them.

My favorite was the Hokey Pokey. A group of girls stood in a circle and moved according to the direction of the words of the song; the chorus was,

> You do the hokey pokey,
> And you turn all around.
> You do the hokey pokey,
> And then you touch the ground.
> You do the hokey pokey,
> You do the hokey pokey,
> You do the hokey pokey,
> That's what it's all about.

The verses lasted as long as someone could think of parts of the body. For example,

> You put your right foot in,
> You put your right foot out,
> You put your right foot in,
> And you shake it all about.

We sang the chorus after each verse, sometimes doing the whole song two or three times before we tired of the game.

We also played a game of tag called Little Sally Walker. We stood in a circle with our eyes closed and chanted,

> Little Sally Walker,
> Sitting in the saucer,
> Rise, Sally, rise.
> Wipe your weeping eyes.
> Put your hand on your hip,
> And let your backbone slip.
> Oh, shake it to the east,
> And shake it to the west,
> Shake it to the one that
> You love the best.

At that point, the person in the center who was "it" — Little Sally Walker — touched someone and tried to run back to her spot in the circle before she was tagged by the one touched.

Songs were a big part of our games. Instead of counting to measure time for Hide and Seek, we sang,

> Last night,
> And the night before,
> Twenty-four robbers at my door.
> I got up and let them in.
> Hit them in the head
> With the rolling pin.

The person who was "it" chanted this until he didn't get a reply to the question, "All hide?" (One of our friends from Texas always said, "Shall I kill him?" instead of "All hide?")

Then began the litany of places where the hiders could not hide.

"Anybody on base is out."

"Anybody in the house is out."

"Anybody in a tree is out."

"Anybody off the block is out." (That one was hard to prove.)

When the seeker had excluded almost every place there was to hide, he then sang out, "Here I come, ready or not."

Along with these gentle games came our apprenticeship as storytellers. We took our lead from our parents on the front porch in the evenings and added our own imagination and sense of place. Our parents told stories from their childhoods in the southern states; we told stories that took place in St. Paul, right on our block, and some of them became a part of the life of the place. One such story was about the cats and dogs in the neighborhood.

People in my neighborhood didn't keep pets in the 1930s, except hunting dogs, of course. Cats were just a part of the outdoors, like squirrels and birds, roaming all over the neighborhood and sometimes disappearing for weeks at a time. Dogs settled in garages or sheds near people who fed them until they were chased off, often by one of their benefactor's kids.

But these things only applied to *real* cats and dogs. We knew from listening to the grown-ups that dead people came back to haunt the earth as cats and dogs. And our block had a lot of cats and dogs that weren't real, because it contained Neal's Funeral Home, facing Rondo.

It was important to know the difference between a real dog and a ghost dog because sometimes real dogs bite. Fortunately, we had a foolproof way, no matter how far away they were. When we saw a cat or dog, we closed our eyes and slowly counted to five. If the animal was still there when we opened our eyes, it was real. If it was gone, it had been a ghost.

Using this technique, we all saw plenty of ghosts. We tried to match the cat or dog to someone who had recently died, then to guess which neighbor they had come back to haunt.

I don't know about the other kids, but I don't count to five anymore. When I see a cat or a dog coming toward me, I just casually blink.

In the wintertime the street games gave way to ice and snow games. "War" was a glorified snowball fight with a snow fort and stockpiles of snowballs. Someone always poured water over the snowballs to make ice balls. It's a wonder that we didn't end up brain damaged, because when one of those ice balls connected with your head, you saw stars.

Everyone had a pair of ice skates — used, and either too big or too small, but we were happy to have them. And without real hockey sticks, pucks, or protective gear, we played hockey during the winter months in the Hollow.

The Hollow was as much a part of our lives as family, church, and school. It was an open space located in the square block between Kent and Mackubin and St. Anthony and Central. It did not fill the entire block, but rather took up fourteen lots (seven facing Central and seven facing St. Anthony) near the middle of the block between Kent and Mackubin, directly across the street from my house. On the St. Anthony side it was lower than the sidewalk, and if there had once been steps leading down to the level part, they were gone by my time. A high chain fence ran around three sides, with a gate opening onto St. Anthony; on the fourth side, the Central side, was a long low building used in the early 1930s as the warming house for an ice skating rink. During the years when I was small, black children were not permitted to use the rink—except for Mrs. Neal's son Andrew and another neighborhood boy. They had the after-school job of sweeping the rink before it was reflooded.

Mrs. Neal did everything she could to get the rink integrated, but the owners would not consider it. She argued that since it was located in our neighborhood, we should have access. They insisted that they would lose business if they allowed "colored" people to skate there. Mrs. Neal made Andrew quit the job and she told the owners that since only white people could skate there, they'd better find a white boy to clean it up. I went to sleep in the wintertime with the sound of the organ music playing for the skaters. And when I was a little older I could go across the street and watch them through the chain link fence.

I don't know exactly what happened, but by the time I was eight or nine, the skating rink moved out and the gates were literally opened for the neighborhood. In winter, a rink was flooded for skating and hockey; in spring, summer, and fall we played baseball, football, volleyball (without a net), and kickball.

The Hollow held four playing fields, plus plenty of room for horseshoe beds along the sidelines. When more than one baseball game was going on at the same time the balls would sometimes get mixed up. You've never seen such confusion. Base hits easily turn into home runs while there was an argument about which ball belonged in which game.

But it was a perfect place to play. At least once a summer the Hollow was filled with one of the little neighborhood carnivals that set themselves up on empty lots. It took three or four days to charm all of the "extra" money out of that neighborhood. Aunt Good would take a turn talking about not having any extra money, yet Morris and Oscar were always able to give me enough to go to the carnival.

Because it was also an easy place for parents to find us, the whole neighborhood loved the Hollow. Winter and summer, right about dusk, you could hear parents calling their children in for the night from the Hollow.

Since none of us was allowed to visit other people's houses after dark, "only" children lost their companions when the sun went down. Girls spent most of the long winter evenings in indoor activities learning the crafts of womanhood. And, of course, the radio serials like "Jack Armstrong, the All-American Boy," "The Lone Ranger," and "The Shadow" were after-supper entertainment.

By the time we were ten or eleven, we were invited to play the real street games with the older children. These games, unlike the ones attached to songs, were tough and competitive. Being pretty and coquettish was not a part of them. When we played games like Red Rover, it took real strength because that game is won by being able to judge both your own and your opponents' weakest link.

The game started with two captains (they didn't seem to be picked; everyone knew who the captains would be) who chose the teams. There were about a dozen kids in our block and usually someone visiting, so we had pretty good-sized teams. The boys were always picked first, then Tomboy, who was the strongest of the girls, and then the other girls. At first I was picked last. Since I was small in size, I had to concentrate on what I was doing in order to be a good player; as time when on and I learned the tricks of the game, I was at least up there with the strong girls. The teams faced each other, about twenty feet apart, each player hanging on to his teammates' wrists to form a strong and — we hoped — unbreakable link. Then one team would figure out who was the weakest player on the other team and call him over: "Red Rover, Red Rover, send Carl McDaniels over!" Carl looked at the opposing team, decided which was the weakest link, and ran with all his might to try to break through. If he did, he returned to his team. If he didn't, he joined the other team. The game was over when all the players were on one team.

I mention Red Rover because, more than any other game that we played, it established our individual places in the community. We gained the reputations that were to follow us into adulthood. Gene, large and strong, was a team player with absolute loyalty. Earl, good looking and popular with the girls, took advantage of this popularity when he chose a spot to break through. Tomboy — Toni Stone — always picked the hardest point to break through and when she grew up she became the first woman to play professional baseball, joining the Negro Leagues in the 1940s. Blanche, gentle Blanche, did not let the opponents know of her real strength until it was too late. Carl, the neighborhood clown, used humor to relax the opponents, and then burst through. The politicians chose their friends to break through, the pretty girls chose the boys, the bullies picked the weak links. The rest of us were operating on just plain guts. The "sissies" in the neighborhood didn't play Red Rover. If you were suspected of letting a bully or a friend through, you were banned from the game for days. That was a major offense in our neighborhood.

Of course, there was "pie," played with knives in the dirt, and hopscotch and jump rope, which we could not play on Sundays because we were wearing our good shoes. Jump rope started out as a nonthreatening game, but by the time we were ten years old and a second rope had been

Neighborhood friends Gene Goss and Blanche Everson, pictured here about 1945

added, along with "hot peppers"—the turners turn the rope as fast as they can—we ended up with as many bruises from it as we did from roller skating.

Marbles was one of my favorite street games. I preferred to play with boys rather than with girls. Boys always played marbles for keeps, but girls wanted to play for fun. I always kept the marbles I had won—after all, I didn't ask for mine back when I lost.

There were diversions from playing, of course. Besides our household chores, there was our religious training. Most of the black kids from the larger neighborhood spent every summer morning at the Summer Bible School sponsored by the Welcome Hall on Farrington and St. Anthony.

Welcome Hall Community Center had been added to

the Zion Presbyterian Church, which was sponsored by several white Presbyterian congregations. Only a few of the children who used the community center were members of Zion. The majority of us came from the other churches in St. Paul. The Catholic kids didn't come, of course, and we teased them about missing all the good times that we had. We hoped this would pay them back for leaving school once a week for their religious training and coming late on their holy days.

Just coming and going to Summer Bible School was fun. The Welcome Hall was seven or eight blocks from my house. During these walks we practiced Pig Latin and Carnival talk, which we used to keep secrets from adults, or so we thought.

Bible School began and ended with chapel, which was really only a song. In the morning we sang, "Praise God from Whom All Blessings Flow," and after school we sang, "May the Good Lord Bless and Keep You, 'Til We Meet Again."

The classes were like Sunday school except that we did craft projects based on the liturgical year. We also had recess at the Welcome Hall playground. I didn't care much for the playground because there was always a threat of being hurt. Someone would get off the teeter-totter when you were in the air, or push you off the swing when you were up really high, or worse yet, dare you to swing so high that you went over the top of the pole. I hated going over the top of the pole, but being called chicken was worse.

It seems that everything I did outside my home during the first decade of my life was based on the Bible. The schoolteachers did not preach religion, but the Christmas, Thanksgiving, and Easter holidays were certainly religious. It was expected that children were to receive a religious education in addition to their academic studies. Although Mama had been gone for two years and I had left her church, I certainly had not left religion.

Now it was time for me to prepare to go to the Summer
Bible School Camp sponsored by the Welcome Hall at
Snail Lake. Since the boys and girls went to camp at different times, the little girls at last had a real opportunity to
experience a broader challenge.

12

Camp

I wanted to go to camp when I was nine, and I think I had Aunt Good talked into it, but Morris heard about it and said no.

"Why not? All the other kids are going."

"In the first place, all of the other kids are not going and even if they were, what's that got to do with you going?"

I knew I had made a mistake. Morris always said, "Just because all of the other kids are jumping off a bridge, does that mean that you'll jump off the bridge, too?"

"Why can't I go?"

"Evelyn, you can't go because you haven't learned to take care of yourself yet."

"What do you mean, I don't take care of myself? I take care of myself all the time."

"No, you don't. When you're at home, we take care of you. When you're in school or church the teachers and grown-ups take care of you. And besides that, the kids in this neighborhood don't do a lot of fighting."

"I'm not going to fight."

"I know that, and that's why you can't go to camp. Some of those kids that go to Bible School are from Deep Rondo and most of those kids love to fight."

Morris was right about that. They didn't do much fighting in Bible School because the teachers were always there. But every time the teachers weren't looking, somebody got hit. I liked the kids from Deep Rondo. I had met all of them in school, but since they didn't walk to school the same way I did, I didn't really hang out with them. I got to know them a lot better at Bible School. I had always thought they were poorer than we were, but that wasn't true. We were all poor. Our houses and yards were bigger, but they seemed to have more money than we did. They also made more noise and got in more trouble than we did, but then, those of us who lived in the middle ground of the black neighborhood made more noise and got in more trouble than the kids who lived father up the way on Oatmeal Hill.

The kids from Deep Rondo and those from our neighborhood had one thing in common: we both disliked the stuck-up kids who lived on Oatmeal Hill. The kids from my neighborhood knew the kids from Oatmeal Hill because most of them had lived in our neighborhood until recently, and we went to the same churches and to the Hallie Q. Brown Community House on Kent and Aurora. The Oatmeal Hill kids went to Maxfield grade school instead of McKinley, where most of the rest of us went, so there was little opportunity for the kids who lived in Deep Rondo to meet them.

Hallie Q. Brown sponsored a camp also, which most of the kids from Oatmeal Hill went to. It was considered more elite because the parents had to pay a fee, while Snail Lake was fully subsidized. But I liked the kids I went to camp with, so even though a lot of our parents could have paid after the war brought more money into our lives, we chose to stay with Snail Lake Camp, the camp for the poor kids.

I said most of this to Morris to try to convince him that I would be among friends and that there was nothing to worry about. It didn't work.

"Evelyn, you've never had a real fight in your life and I'm not going to let you go out there to camp with a bunch of rough kids."

The following spring, when I was ten, I had my test of fire. Harry lived next door to the empty lot on our block, which was halfway between our house and school. He was one of the "cute" boys in my grade, and he could have been popular if he weren't such a bully to girls and younger boys. Although he was not a large boy, he was certainly bigger than I was. At some point that spring he had decided to threaten to beat me up every day after school as I passed his house on the way home. If I came up the alley, he was in his backyard. If I came up the street, he was sitting on the front step leaning against the door. When he started threatening me, I ran home as fast as I could. As soon as I got within sight of my house, he stopped chasing me, but always with a promise to catch me the next day.

One day he almost caught me, so I started going out of my way around the block to get home. This worked fine until Aunt Good saw me coming home from the wrong direction and asked me why.

"I was just walking some of my friends up Rondo. It's not really out of the way."

"What do you mean, it's not out of the way? You're coming from the opposite direction of the school, and you're trying to tell me it's not out of the way?"

"No, it's not out of the way, Aunt Good."

"Evelyn, it's out of the way. You know you're supposed to come straight home from school. If something would happen to you up on Rondo, I wouldn't even know where you were. It's out of the way and you know it's out of the way and I don't want you coming home that way any more. Get in the house and change your clothes."

All the next day in school I worried about what I was going to do. Harry saw me on the playground and asked me what had happened to me after school, so I knew he was still waiting for me by his house. I also knew that Aunt Good was usually in the house when I came home from school so I could come the roundabout way and she proba-

bly wouldn't see me. I could go past our house and if she
came out I would be coming from the right direction. This
sounded like a good plan to me, since I couldn't think of
a second lie to tell about why I was coming from the wrong
direction.

It was a good plan, but it didn't work because Aunt
Good was standing on the front porch waiting for me and
as soon as I passed Mrs. Garret's high picket fence she saw
me. She just stood there on the porch with her hands on
her hips and waited for me to get to the house and up the
stairs. I headed for the door, but she stepped in front of it.

"Evelyn, where are you going?"

"In the house to change my clothes, Aunt Good."

"Didn't I tell you yesterday not to come home from
school that way?"

"Yes, ma'am."

"Then why did you come that way again?"

"I don't know."

By now the tears had welled up in my eyes. I didn't
know what to do. I just stood there, looking down.

"What's the matter with you? Standing there crying
and lying about coming home the wrong way. What's the
matter with you?"

I really started crying hard now.

"Come on in this house. You're going to tell me what's
the matter with you or I'm going to beat you to death."

That really scared me. Aunt Good rarely threatened to
spank me, because Mama had spanked me so often, but she
didn't offer any empty threats, either. She intended to find
out why I was coming home the wrong way. So I told her.
She had no sympathy for me.

"If you walk out of your way to avoid a fight, you'll be
doing that all of your life."

"No, I won't, Aunt Good."

"I know you won't, 'cause you're going to face this one."

"He's bigger than I am, and he's a boy."

"Everybody's bigger than you are, Evelyn. Size doesn't make any difference. The bigger they come, the harder they fall. Tomorrow, you're going to fight that boy or come home and fight me. Take your choice."

That evening when Morris and Oscar came home, the three of them gave me pointers on how to fight a boy who was bigger and stronger than I was. It didn't do any good. All I could think about was Harry beating me up. I had another bad day in school trying to choose between Aunt Good beating me or Harry beating me. It wasn't just Aunt Good, it was also the scorn I would receive from my two older brothers. By the end of the day, I had chosen Harry.

As I cleared the empty lot, Harry got up from the step as usual, but instead of running as I always did, I stopped. He walked toward me real slow, threatening me with every step. I was so scared I couldn't hear anything he said, I just knew that when he got close to me he was going to beat me up. So when he got right in front of me, I hit him and I kept on hitting him, because I knew that if I stopped hitting him he was really going to get me. And while I was hitting him I was screaming at the top of my voice because I was so scared he was going to start beating me up. I don't know how it happened, but we were on the ground and I was still hitting him and screaming when Aunt Good pulled me off of him.

"He's not going to bother you anymore, Ba'. You can stop hitting him now."

There were a lot of people standing around when Aunt Good and I went home.

"No, sir, I don't think you'll have any more trouble from that little boy."

Of course, I didn't believe her at the time, but Harry wasn't waiting for me on his step anymore after that.

That summer when I asked again to go to camp after Summer Bible School was over, Morris said, "Yeah, we might as well let you go, you can take care of yourself now."

From a city girl's perspective, the campground seemed to be endless. It had electricity and indoor plumbing; other than that, it was pretty primitive. There was a small boathouse by the pier. Up the hill from the lake was the lodge that held the sleeping quarters on the second floor, a large meeting room on the first, and the mess hall in the basement. There was also a bathhouse (without hot water), a large campfire circle, a hand pump where we got all of our drinking water during the day, a baseball diamond, a volleyball court (with a net), horseshoe beds, and picnic tables. All of this was surrounded by a forest with cleared paths that were used for nature-study field trips.

I never went to any other camp, but I suppose that what we did was standard camp activity. Our days began at 6:00 A.M. with a morning dip in the cold water of Snail Lake. In between meals, which began with the first few lines of "Praise God from Whom All Blessings Flow," were scheduled crafts, sports, and, of course, Bible study. Dr. Crump came to the camp each year to give us a class on sex education, which consisted mostly of birth control (abstinence) and avoidance of venereal disease (abstinence).

As my very first week of camp passed, an aching secret pain spread from my stomach to the rest of my body. Sunday was Visitors' Day, and I had told Aunt Good and Morris not to come and see me. "After all, I'll only be gone two weeks. Hardly any of the other parents are coming. The other kids would probably tease me if you came up to see me after only one week."

I really meant that when I said it. But as the week passed, I thought surely I would die before the two weeks were up. I couldn't tell anyone how I was feeling, but as Sunday approached, I had decided to ask one of the other parents to take me home, because Aunt Good and my brothers were missing me so much.

Sunday finally came and more parents than I had expected came to visit. I kept running around and playing with the kids who didn't have visitors yet, but I didn't miss one car that came down that road from the highway, hoping to see someone who lived close to me. Finally I gave up and walked down by the lake, because I was afraid that I might start crying. I wished I didn't cry when I felt sad. Aunt Good always called me "Chicken Heart" because I cried so easily.

I was sitting down by the dock wishing that I had never heard of camp, when I heard Morris say, "Ba', what you doing down here all by yourself?"

I jumped up and ran to Morris, tears washing my face, hugging him and then Aunt Good.

"Girl, what are you crying for?"

"I didn't think you were going to come. I didn't think you were going to come. I didn't think you were going to come."

"We told you we were going to come on visiting day."

"Yeah, but I told you not to come."

"Girl, we don't pay no attention to what you tell us."

"Come on now, stop crying and show us around the camp."

They spent a few hours with me and by the time they left I didn't ask to go home with them. Camp was fun again.

Friday nights we had our campfire meeting, where we sang songs and told stories. At about a quarter to eleven, we went into the dorm, put on our pajamas, and said our prayers. At a few minutes before eleven one of the counselors turned out the lights and another turned the radio on to "Lights Out," a program that used the sense of sound to scare the living daylights out of its listeners. It was produced to be listened to in the dark, and its tones drove our imaginations to new depths of horror each week.

Sometimes at home I was allowed to stay up and hear the program, but "Lights Out" at home was nothing like "Lights Out" at camp. The real fear there was in knowing that somebody was creeping around the dormitory ready to grab us. Sure enough, toward the end of the program, someone would scream, and then everyone else would scream and the counselors would turn the lights on and try to find out who had done the grabbing. They never did. We all thought it was one of the counselors; but then again, we were never sure.

My turn didn't come until my last year at camp. I was sitting up in bed listening to the program and listening for the creeper at the same time. The program got so scary that little by little it took my full attention. And then I heard the girl in the next bed breathing and I thought she was scared too. But the breathing got louder and closer, and then it was right beside my bed, and it didn't go away. I kept waiting for the person to grab me, but it never did. It just kept breathing a little closer all the time. I didn't know what to do. I was afraid to move, even to put my head under the cover. I knew it was a ghost. But I didn't believe in ghosts anymore, not even the one in the lake. When I saw something I told everyone it was a big fish or maybe a turtle, 'cause there weren't any ghosts. But what if there *were* ghosts and the one in the lake got mad at me for not believing in it and had come to get me? Oh! God! It was a ghost! It was the ghost in the lake! I had to look. So I turned around real fast and bumped into it and it laughed and laughed. And the other kids laughed and screamed and someone turned the lights on, and it was one of the counselors laughing and laughing. And she sat on my bed and laughed and laughed until she cried.

"Boy! Were you scared! You stopped breathing, you were so scared." And she started laughing all over again.

By now I was getting embarrassed. So I said, "You didn't scare me. I knew it was you all the time." And I *should* have known that it was the counselors. They were the only ones who weren't scared to get out of bed. Still, just before I went to sleep I thought, "Maybe there is a ghost in the lake after all. How do I know? . . . Naw, there's no such things as ghosts."

Going to camp gave us something to write about on the first day of school when the teacher asked us for an essay on "What I Did Last Summer." But it was more important than that. We didn't know the few black farmers in the state, and none of our families could afford a lake cabin. Camp was the only opportunity most of us had to experience country life in Minnesota.

13

Taylor's Musical Strings

Mr. and Mrs. Taylor were a middle-aged Negro couple without children who wanted to enrich the lives of young Negro girls left without parents. They chose music as their tool. This was odd, since neither of them had any musical skills. As it turned out, musical skill was not necessary for two people who had a sense of purpose.

Eva Taylor's skill was her patience. She wasn't really good with children, in the traditional way, but she could outlast any antics that we could think of with good humor and dignity. It took only a few weeks for us to understand that her patience was limitless and that we were just wasting our own time.

William Taylor worked as a Pullman porter for the Pullman Company, but on his off days he became the world's most creative promoter. He encouraged a few girls to join the band and those few encouraged the rest of us. He bought, borrowed, and begged enough stringed instruments for us to use, and he hired Mr. Albert Bellson, of Bellson Music Company in downtown St. Paul, to give weekly instruction in classical music.

One day when I was about ten, Martha Hilyard, who lived with her family on Central Avenue near Kent Street, came by my house to ask me if I wanted to play in the Taylors' band.

My answer was automatically yes. "I'll go ask Aunt Good."

Aunt Good, not being as quick as I to jump at a new opportunity, started asking Martha all kinds of dumb questions, like,

"Who's got this band?"

"Mr. and Mrs. Taylor."

"Who are they?"

"They live up on St. Anthony by Maxfield school."

"They got a phone?"

"Yes, ma'am."

"Next time you go there, give them my number and tell them to call me. They ain't got no business sending a child to talk to a grown person, anyway."

Realizing that this wasn't going the way it was supposed to, Martha quickly backtracked.

"She didn't *send* me, Mrs. Keaton, I just mentioned Evelyn and she asked me to see about it."

Martha and I could tell by Aunt Good's face that we would only make matters worse by continuing to talk. So Martha got our phone number and left.

Mrs. Taylor called Aunt Good the next week. And after a long conversation, Aunt Good was finally satisfied and told Mrs. Taylor I could come the next week and we'd see how it worked out.

There were two black female string bands in St. Paul at the time. Mr. Mym Carter, a local music teacher, started the other one among his students. They played "worldly" music. The blues played by a group of talented young musicians on several stringed instruments is a sound you won't soon forget, or ever describe. Our band, Taylor's Musical Strings, played classical, folk, and gospel music. Gospel played by a group of talented young musicians on several stringed instruments is a sound you won't soon forget, or ever describe, either.

There was a strong friendly sense of competition between the bands, kept alive by constant teasing. Opportunities to tease were many since we went to the same schools, churches, community centers, and, of course, camps. The teasing didn't stop us from getting together for "jam sessions," and during those sessions both Mr. Carter and Mr. Bellson would have been proud of us. We were good.

It didn't take us long to notice that all of the members of our band were orphans. At that time, the category included any child who had lost one of her natural parents. By now Blanche's father had died, so she could join the band, too.

The Taylors gave us each an instrument and bought the strings we were constantly breaking during those early months. Our schedule was steady and strict. Mr. Bellson gave us technical instruction once a week. While the rest of the band practiced in the kitchen of the Taylors' house, he took each instrument section upstairs to the spare bedroom for a private lesson before rehearsing us all together.

First I played the guitar, and later the mandocello. The mandocello is a fretted instrument the size of a guitar with three double strings, like the mandolin, and a single bass string. Music is written for it in the bass clef. It has the rich tone of the cello and the versatility and range of the mandolin. Now and then a solo part was written for it; but mainly, it could be compared to the alto voice.

Blanche played the second mandolin, Martha the guitar, Alice and Mildred (sisters and old friends from the Sanctified church) mandola and guitar. Barbara Jean, another band member, also played the mandolin. Viola (who dressed and acted strange) played the best bass guitar in town.

Besides the lessons, we practiced twice a week with Mrs. Taylor. To play the music as written, we had to ignore her because she used her baton to draw a triangle in the air in three-quarter time, no matter what we were playing.

It was very different when Mr. Bellson led the band. He

*Evelyn (right) and Mildred Gude about 1945,
a few years after they played together in Taylor's
Musical Strings*

stood in front of us looking at the music on the stand. Then
he raised both hands chest-high with his elbows sticking
out. He looked at each of us, one at a time, to make sure
he had our attention. Then he made the slightest movement with his baton and we started to play. Even if your
instrument was not one of the beginning instruments,
when the song started, you started to "play."

With his hands, his head, his winged arms, his facial expressions, and sometimes his entire body, he made us play the song the way he felt it should be played. When he led us in one of Sousa's marches, he created an entire parade for us to play for. And when we played the lullaby "Mighty Like a Rose," it seemed he almost fell asleep before we tiptoed to the final measure.

Because we were too young to know our limitations, we all soon knew how to read music in both clefs, play our primary instrument very well, play a second instrument well enough, and bluff on all the other instruments. In fact, when we started performing, our show stopper was to play our theme song, "What a Friend We Have in Jesus," rotating instruments until we had all played each. It took four choruses to rotate the instruments, and during the second chorus someone would minor a chord here, augment another there, run a riff between phrases, or double or halve the timing, giving the melody a definite blues sound. We did it mainly to aggravate Mrs. Taylor, who always remembered the instruments that did it, but never remembered who was playing that instrument at the time.

She always wondered where we had learned the blues techniques. We certainly didn't learn them from Mr. Bellson. She trusted us so much that she didn't suspect that when we took our instruments home to practice, we weren't necessarily practicing the music we played for our programs.

We were so eager to learn the popular new songs that we copied them from the records we had at home. This was not too difficult, because all we had to do was figure out the key, and, using our knowledge of musical patterns, reproduce the sounds. It also helped that most of us had come out of the Sanctified and Southern Baptist churches, because the beat and sway of gospel are very similar to the blues. And I suppose it helped that we jammed with the other band.

Of course, it was simpler for some than others. Alice, Mildred, and Viola were natural musicians, so they only had to hear music once to reproduce it. But I had very little natural ability, so I had to take every chord or riff apart and then put it back together again. When one of the natural musicians played it with me, I'd get it "right." The natural musicians helped the others, but those of us without that talent knew more about music. We had to.

We played together for a little over four years. After the first year we began to be paid. With the first monies, the Taylors bought our uniforms. They were actually majorette uniforms: dark and light blue trimmed in red, with red satin-lined waist-length capes that we threw over our left shoulders when we played. Viola insisted on throwing hers over her right shoulder.

After the uniforms were bought, we were paid in twenty-five-cent U.S. savings stamps, one stamp for each performance. That was not a small thing. We were the only children in the neighborhood with savings. The money began to mount up, too, because we played for churches, settlement houses, family reunions, and celebrations of different kinds, and twice we played on the radio at the Minnesota State Fair. Our golden moment came when we played for a men's convention at the St. Paul Hotel.

We played most of Stephen Foster's songs, Sousa marches, and, because our training was classical, a lot of Bach. The official Negro National Anthem, "Lift Every Voice and Sing," was requested the most. We thought James Weldon Johnson was the composer, but he only wrote the lyrics; his brother J. Rosamond Johnson wrote the music. That song has everything for a musician. It's full-bodied, with important parts for all the instruments. The rhythm and tempo are varied, the shading and phrasing are intricate, the figuring is difficult, requiring the purest tones, and you never get it quite right. Nothing pleases musicians more than finding music that constantly presses them to play better the next time. In most songs, the first mandolins had the melody, but this song gave the melody line to the mandocello, to imitate a rich baritone vocal solo. Although we didn't sing the words, we put those words into our playing. There was no doubt what this song was all about, even if you'd never heard of it before. This is not a song about Ol' Black Joe hoping to receive his reward in heaven. It's a song of pride, joy, and resolve.

We also played all of the old spirituals and slave songs, and so we were popular with almost any group. We were popular, and we were good. That's all Mr. Taylor needed to put his promotional skills to work. On the way to the performances in the bus Mr. Taylor had "acquired," the Taylors told us about their dreams for us and how proud they were, and they listed the advantages of being trained and experienced musicians. And we glowed with self-assurance and arrogance and played better than ever.

Then one day, all at once (or so it seemed), we discovered boys. First, the uniforms no longer fit us. The outfits that we had been so proud of as children were now confining to those longed-for swellings of womanhood. Mrs. Taylor offered to buy larger sizes for the girls who were "growing." Of course, this suggestion was refused. The Taylors didn't realize that we had entered the day of the sweater girl, and there was no uniform in the world that could satisfy us. Then we insisted on wearing high heels and silk stockings rather than the oxfords and the blue socks that matched our dresses. We couldn't rehearse on nights when there was a high school football game. We couldn't perform on weekend afternoons because that's when the boys were at the drugstore. And at the same time, our social consciousness grew and we called Mr. and Mrs. Taylor "Uncle Toms" and refused to play songs like "Ol' Black Joe" or the intricate jigs and reels that were such favorites with our white audiences. The band began to break up, player by player, and I had dropped out before Taylor's Musical

Strings made its last formal appearance, in Chicago. All together, it took us about three months to break up the band and the hearts of Mr. and Mrs. Taylor.

Later, the Taylors tried to start another band with younger children, but their money was gone, their patience with beginning players was gone, and we had aged them so much their spirit was gone, too. The new band didn't work. By the time we were mature enough to realize what we had done, not only to the Taylors but to our own musical careers, it was too late. The time for it to happen had passed.

14

The War

By the time I entered high school, World War II was a part of our lives. The war had started for me in 1939, when our grade school participated in "Bundles for Britain," a national program to aid the British war effort. The girls in our sixth grade were taught to knit six-inch squares, which the teacher sewed together to make afghans to be sent to the wounded soldiers in England. The boys in the class sold small household items and used the profits to purchase the yarn and pay the postage.

Although I knitted my share, Aunt Good, who liked to knit, not only furnished yarn but knitted constantly that winter. I won the prize for furnishing the most squares for the afghans. School prizes were always writing tablets, which were highly valued by the students. The cost of the tablets—a nickel—was not a small sum to parents, and we were forbidden to use the paper from our regular tablets for anything other than schoolwork until the end of the school year.

As the war progressed, I went from grade school to high school and from anklets to silk stockings. At least, I would have worn silk stockings, but a wonderful thing happened. The supply of silk from Japan was cut off—silk that was needed for parachutes. Older women switched to rayon, but young women wore leg makeup and lace stockings: wonderful adult-looking lace stockings. Wonderful adult-looking black lace stockings with ankle-strapped high-heeled shoes.

High school girls were encouraged to write to the boys in the armed forces, to keep them in touch with home. We met them by putting our names and addresses in the magazines we sent to the United Service Organizations — the USO. By the end of high school, most of the girls were writing to at least four servicemen, and we all had great fun sharing those letters with each other. Except for Rachel. Rachel was the girl in our school who didn't fit.

Teenagers cast exact molds of what people should look like, what they should wear, and how they should talk. Rachel was different. She was not fat, but she was a big girl, with a big head and a big face full of big teeth. Her short, thin hair looked like a wig that was a size too small. Most of her body weight was in her shoulders and chest, leaving very little for her hips and legs, and at the bottom of her little legs were large, square feet that didn't match her hands at all. Her hands, though large, were smooth and well formed and moved with a hypnotic rhythm that sometimes caused you to forget what the rest of her looked like.

Rachel lived with her grandmother and we often said that she and her grandmother wore the same clothes. She wore plain dresses belted at the waist and polished leather shoes while the rest of us were wearing large sweaters, short skirts, and dirty saddle oxfords with two pairs of bobby socks that matched our sweaters and skirts in color.

But her worst offense was her speech. Rachel was intelligent, with a vocabulary twice the size of ours, and she pronounced all of her words correctly with a slight British accent that never faltered. She never spoke what was to become known as black English. She was also arrogant. The teachers, of course, appreciated her good manners and scholarship, and they rewarded her with good grades and special favors. There was nothing about her that we accepted or liked. We either avoided her or tried to chip away at that arrogance, which we did with a certain amount of success.

Because of Rachel's literary skills and lack of social life, she wrote to many more servicemen than the rest of us. All went well until one of the young men fell for Rachel, or at least her ability to write letters, and asked her for a picture. She sent him a picture, but it wasn't of herself. It was one she had exchanged with one of the class beauties, one of the white class beauties. None of us knew about this picture-swapping until he wrote to her saying he was coming to see her on his next furlough with the intention of asking for her hand in marriage. One day at the lunch table Rachel confessed her dilemma to us, because she needed our advice. Our first response was to laugh.

"I knew you kids were going to laugh at me. I should never have told you in the first place."

Rachel's superior attitude had cost her friends among the students, but she certainly couldn't go to any of the teachers and tell them she had been dishonest. She was stuck with us. And we were very unsympathetic.

"I suppose you told him you were rich, too."

"Well, I didn't exactly say that I was rich. But I told him some things that would make him think I was rich."

"Things like what, Rachel?"

"Well, I told him of the new saddle I had acquired, for one thing."

That started another round of laughter.

At first her face didn't change as the tears filled her eyes. Then she blinked and water was everywhere, on her clothes, on the table, on the backs of her hands and arms when she wiped her face. She opened her mouth and all of those teeth poked out and with them a strange sound from somewhere in her body. We stopped laughing, of course, and watched her as she looked from one to another of us, making that funny sound with her body, kind of jerking, and her big mouth open and that water coming from everywhere, her eyes, her nose, and her mouth. No one wanted to touch her 'cause she looked so horrible, but we did try to get her to stop crying. When she got enough control to talk, the British accent was gone and so was the "proper" speech.

"You guys, whattammy gonna do?"

As hard as we tried, we couldn't stop ourselves from one more round of laughter. We had finally won, we had broken Rachel. But that meant that the fun was gone. We didn't like her any better, but at least now we felt sorry for her. We also were interested in her predicament, so we had a good time helping her get out of it. Since she was unwilling to tell him the truth—somehow we all understood why—the only way to get out of one lie was to tell another one. So we helped her come up with a story about how her family was sending her to Europe to study for a year, and we suggested that she bring the correspondence to a close.

Later, there was something about Rachel's walk that told us she wasn't writing to her pen pal any more, and her new quiet told us she had not regained her arrogance. And much later, as we matured, we realized that this was not a funny story. In fact, it was one of the sad stories of the war for these two young people.

The good times of the war for us were the monthly USO dances with a live big band at the naval air station near Wold-Chamberlain Field. Girls sixteen and older gathered at community centers, where buses picked them up and took them to the dances.

We didn't go to more than half a dozen of these dances, yet I have vivid memories of the bus rides out to Wold-Chamberlain Field, the hours of dancing in a large auditorium with young men (not schoolboys), to beautiful wartime songs like "I'll Be Seeing You" and "Do Nothing Till You Hear It from Me," and the return bus rides. Some of the men, along with their commanding officers and our chaperones, rode back with us, singing the songs that we

Students at Mechanic Arts High School in St. Paul looking at a map on D-Day, June 6, 1944

had danced to and making promises for dances the next month.

I also did volunteer work in Minneapolis for Operation Skywatch. Skywatch volunteers in Minnesota outside the Twin Cities spotted and identified planes, then called the information in to a building on Lake Street. We plotted the courses of the planes on large maps on the walls. It may seem ludicrous in a time when we can destroy a plane long before it comes into view, but we thought we were helping to keep the country safe by sighting planes in the middle of the country. There were no enemy planes, of course. And at the end of the war, I received a thank-you letter from Hubert H. Humphrey, then mayor of Minneapolis, for my work.

In many ways, the war had been wonderful. Although I saw the gold- and silver-starred banners hanging in front windows of homes in my neighborhood, no one I knew very well died in the war. The blackout exercises that we practiced were more like a game than serious preparation for the bombs that we saw in the movies. Blacks who did not enlist and were not drafted found new jobs in plants manufacturing war goods, new jobs left behind by white servicemen. Everyone had the money to purchase a better life. Our world was broadened by the tales told by young men who had gone to fight the war and brought us back bits and pieces of languages they had learned in Italy, France, Germany, and the South Pacific islands that we had known only through Dorothy Lamour movies.

The depression was over, and now the war was over. The future for young people, especially young black people living in the North, had never held better promise.

15

The Teens

As we became teenagers, we took jobs that forced us to relinquish the Hollow and its games to the younger kids. Because child-labor laws were not strictly enforced, in part due to the labor shortage, there were plenty of jobs for kids under sixteen.

Girls did house cleaning and baby-sitting. Boys on our block could get delivery jobs at the four grocery stores in our neighborhood: White Front and Black's Grocery on Kent and St. Anthony (we always laughed at that because the White Front was owned by Jewish people and Black's was owned by black people), and two more on Rondo and Mackubin. Baines Ice and Coal Company and the pool hall hired young boys to help out, and some of the boys helped their fathers at work.

Our social life changed almost without our knowing it. We traded the Saturday afternoon matinee at the Faust Theatre for its Friday night midnight show, so-called because the second picture of the double feature lasted until after midnight. And before the movie, we gathered at the Lounge.

The Lounge was a room in the Hallie Q. Brown Community House where the high school students gathered to dance every Friday evening. The Hallie, named for the national educator, lecturer, and author who died in 1949, was an important part of our neighborhood. It was funded

Staff meeting at the Hallie Q. Brown Community House, 1935. I. Myrtle Carden (seated third from right) served as director between 1929 and 1949.

through the Community Chest (now called the United Way). The St. Paul branch of the Urban League, a national organization formed to gain fair treatment for people who do not have the power to gain it for themselves, had helped to establish the Hallie. The league's sweeping efforts have helped people of all origins, although its focus has been on black communities. And our neighborhood was slowly becoming all black; the few white families that still lived there didn't attend the Hallie's social functions.

Of course, those social functions were what attracted us. The Lounge had all of the latest records. Once again, being pretty was important, but more important was knowing the latest dance step. It certainly was more important than being handsome (the most popular boys were the good dancers, the good-looking ones came in second). Ballroom dancing was popular for the slow dances. It's hard to remember how many times I fell in love circling around the room to Hoagy Carmichael's "Star Dust."

Hardly anyone went steady when I was a teenager. Our parents frowned on it.

"When you see the same boy all the time, sooner or later you run out of things to talk about. And when two young'uns run out of things to talk about, they start giving other people something to talk about."

Even more important, our *peers* did not expect us to settle down to one person until we reached marrying age, which was late teens for girls. So every Friday evening we dressed up (our new school clothes were worn first to the Hallie) and gathered at the Lounge. There were chaperones there, of course, but we liked them and they didn't seem to get in the way.

The Lounge closed at 9:00 P.M., just in time for us to walk the two blocks to the Faust. The theater had three aisles, and we always sat in the fourth row on the right, not because of any law, but because that's where all of our friends were. The management tolerated lots of noise since the theater made most of its money on young people, so the Faust was a fun place to go. Besides, the movies they showed called for noise — cheering for the guys in the white hats during the cowboy movies, cheering when the girl got the boy in the musical comedies, cheering for the good ol' USA in the war movies, and laughing like crazy at Bud Abbott and Lou Costello. Not everyone sat in the fourth row, of course. When a couple began to be serious about each other, or more important, began to be serious about seeing the entire movie, they would sit in one of the other aisles with the quieter white people.

Although the Lounge was the arena where we strutted the boogie-woogie and first exercised our decision-making abilities on important things like which songs would be on

Junior Dramatics Class at the Hallie, about 1937. The instructor (far left) is Gladys Harris.

the jukebox, it was only a small part of the Hallie. We learned modern dance from Janie Bell Murphy, a young woman who was also our volleyball and basketball coach. She was like a big sister to all of us. I don't think there was a girl who went to the Hallie who didn't end up in the shower room having a gabfest with Janie Bell. She talked to us about anything we wanted to discuss, which was mainly boys and school. Sometimes she called us all in to talk about sportsmanship and team playing. In some ways, she was like the high school counselors in the schools today, except she lived in our neighborhood and we knew she "lived the song she sang about," as Mahalia Jackson used to sing.

At the Hallie we learned to fill the gaps in American history — the gaps that told of the part that black Americans played in the building of this country. The history books spoke only of the menial labor of the slaves. They did not mention the inventions with which these workers improved their production. The books did not mention the skills of the men and women who farmed the land, nor the crafts that they had brought from their native Africa. They did not mention the music that had to be passed down through work songs and prayer meetings. Nor did the school books mention the slaves and freedmen who produced an abundance of literature. We read stories written by these black authors and poets like Phyllis Wheatley to supplement Shakespeare and Chaucer and Elizabeth Barrett Browning.

In the Hallie's new gymnasium we first saw the Harlem Globetrotters play basketball when they stopped by to entertain the kids, and when we were older we partied with them at the Dew Drop Inn on Rice Street. It was also in that new gym that the young black musicians reproduced the big band sound that we had all danced to only a few years earlier.

The Hallie Q. Brown did not have the deep religious base of the Welcome Hall. The Welcome Hall was interested in saving our souls for the next life; the Hallie Q. Brown prepared us to function competitively and yet humanely in this one.

As important as the Hallie was in our social lives, our families believed that it was important to keep "our young folks involved" in the churches. While the Hallie developed citizenship as it provided education, entertainment, and physical training, the churches developed a sense of spirituality, stewardship, and service.

My particular service was as a church usher. Teenagers were glad to be active in the churches because it paid the dues for the activities that followed services. Every Sunday, right after church, most of the black teenagers in St. Paul gathered at Fields' drugstore on Rondo and Dale. And we were dressed to kill. When I was sixteen one of my outfits was a grey wool walking suit with a three-quarter-length coat, trimmed from neck to hem with silver fox fur, over a black chiffon long-sleeved blouse. With it I wore a black felt hat with a large grey plume in the back, black patent-

Dressed up on Sunday: Evelyn, about 1945

leather high-heeled shoes, and a black felt purse, and I carried wrist-length white gloves. I mean, we were dressed to kill. The depression was over and we had jobs that produced money. No more hand-me-downs, mama-made dresses, or look-alike clothes made by WPA workers and distributed by the welfare clothing center.

About once a month, we were joined by our peers from Minneapolis. All of them were as involved with the Phyllis Wheatley House as we were with the Hallie. We had met many times, at games when our teams played each other and at dances at both centers.

It was a strange thing about the two sets of kids. We each reflected the clichés about our hometowns, and therein was the attraction for each other. St. Paul, the seat of old money, produced more conservative people. And the people who worked for them were conservative; and the children of the people who worked for them were conservative.

Dance in the Hallie gymnasium, about 1955

On the other hand, Minneapolis, the home of the *nouveau riche*, produced a more progressive type of people. And the people who worked for them were more progressive; and the children of the people who worked for them were more progressive.

So the St. Paul boys were fascinated with the flash and style of the Minneapolis girls, who were always ahead of us in fashion and dance steps. The Minneapolis girls returned the favor by thinking that St. Paul boys were honest and trustworthy and some day would make excellent husbands.

We St. Paul girls were taken with the sheer manliness of the Minneapolis boys who, besides being ahead in dance steps and fashion, had a mystery about them. They, in turn, poured their attention on us because we played coy and hard-to-get. (In truth, we weren't any harder to get than our swinging sisters to the west.) Any service that our churches needed was well worth the price to be a member of that "after-church crowd" at Fields' drugstore on Sunday afternoon to meet those Minneapolis boys. Van White, Minneapolis's first black alderman, was one of those manly teenage boys.

We could also see each other when the Oxford Roller Rink on Selby Avenue was rented for black kids for a roller-skating party, and at baseball games played by black professionals at the Lexington Ball Park on University Avenue. Because major league baseball teams were all-white—Jackie Robinson had not yet broken the racial barrier—black players formed black leagues and traveled around the country to play. Since most of us were involved in sports, it was a big day when the professionals came to town. One year Olympic gold medal winner Jesse Owens, billed as the "fastest man alive," performed at one of these games. He beat a horse running the hundred yard dash and he beat four men running a relay race around the baseball diamond. We were so proud of Jesse Owens, you would have thought that he was a member of our family. We felt the same way about Joe Louis when he beat James Braddock to become the world champion heavyweight boxer.

Although most of our social life took place in groups, we also dated. For me, the privilege of keeping company came at the same time as the responsibility of keeping a job. So when I started working, I also started dating.

Dating, however, was not without its rules. The first rule was that I could date only in the daytime. In the winter this made for very short dates. I can remember the horror of coming out of a matinee after seeing only a "little bit" of the first part of the show again and finding it dark outside. That meant I would lose my dating privileges for a month. But even worse, I was going to get the lecture in front of the boy when he brought me home. How can you keep your cool in front of a boy when you're catching it from your folks? Especially when the only response allowed is "Yes, ma'am" and "No, ma'am." You hoped you would never see him again.

I also lost my dating privileges one Sunday afternoon when I invited my escort into the house to play a game of cards. After only a short time we had a disagreement about a rule of the game. Before anyone in the house realized the seriousness of the disagreement, we were on the floor fighting. Aunt Good broke up the fight and sent the boy home, but not before a lecture about how "any fool can see that you two are not ready to keep company yet." I didn't date him, or anyone else, while I waited to grow up and "know how to keep company."

My neighborhood was a good place to grow up and live. But I lived in a larger society, which was also a learning experience. Sometimes a bitter learning experience.

16

Being Black in Minnesota

I have no desire to rehash the racial issues of the 1930s and 1940s. Most people are aware, at least after the fact, of the institutionalized discrimination against blacks in this country. However, since I have discussed so many aspects of life with my family and in my neighborhood, I would certainly leave the reader with the wrong impression if I didn't mention racial issues at all. The reader would think that I was either blind to the race situation or that I was trying to paint Minnesota as a utopian state for blacks. Neither is true. The simple fact is that when you are a member of a black family living in a black community, race is rarely an issue. It's only when you step outside of that community that you are confronted with and have to learn to deal with it.

When a black child is very young, how that child feels about black people and white people depends on where he or she was born. A man born in a farming village in Africa once told me that he did not know white men existed until he was nine years old. When he first saw one, he was afraid, thinking the man was a black man who was so sick that his skin had turned white. Old people who were about to die had a similar ashen coloring, and children were not allowed to be around them because they might get the disease. When the white man tried to touch my friend, he ran away in terror, much to the amusement of the man. My friend earned graduate degrees from Oxford University in En-

147

gland and now lives in France. He told me that even though he had traveled widely in Europe and the United States, his first impression had not left him; he still did not think of white people as healthy.

I know several black people who were born in the South, "out in the country," and saw very few white people in their childhood. But they certainly knew that they existed. They had heard from the cradle that the white man was to be feared for his violence, and therefore to be avoided whenever possible. It was to escape this violence that they came north.

As a native Minnesotan, I had coexisted with the whites. Their white skin brought no fear of disease or terror of violence. In fact, the close association with them gave me and my peers the opportunity to copy them. We were raised by the "white is right" generation who really believed that if we copied them, we would someday soon be able to enjoy all of the richness of life that was theirs. The stories we heard from the people who worked in private service and the movies we saw kept us well informed about just how grand that life could be.

We watched and studied and copied them in every way possible. We straightened our hair because white people's hair was straight. Many darker-skinned people used Black and White Bleaching Cream on their skin to become closer in color to the whites. We did not wear the bright primary colors that we preferred. We hushed our full voices and we modified our speech patterns to match those of our white neighbors. We denied to the whites that we listened to "the blues," and we accepted the Christian faith. No, we cherished the Christian faith. After all, the basis of the Christian community was brotherly love. When that love seemed to be a little slow in materializing, then we could certainly count on it as the distributor of wings in the life hereafter.

I gotta wings.
You gotta wings.
Alla God's children
Gotta wings.
When I gets to Heaven,
Gonna put on my wings,
And fly all over God's Heaven.
Heaven.
Yes, when I gets to Heaven,
Gonna put on my wings,
And fly all over God's Heaven.

The bottom line was that we knew that the chance for equality lay in our ability to assimilate into the white Christian society. These were the facts.

Like other children, I knew by the time I entered school that not only were there differences among people, but judgments were based on these differences.

This was the simple view of the racial situation. However, even at an early age, I was aware that nothing, not even race issues, is black or white. For example, I knew Democrats were better than Republicans (at least after Roosevelt's election), the Sanctified church was better than any other Protestant church (and Catholicism was not even a religion), and blacks were better than whites. I also knew Republicans *thought* they were better than Democrats, other churches *thought* they were better than the Sanctified church, and whites *thought* they were better than blacks.

These were the complexities of our young lives; yet, despite them, our minds and spirits were kept whole and healthy by the tough-skinned black people like Mama and Daddy who came to Minnesota to find a better life. Open segregation and the daily threat of violence were gone and there was the promise that life for their children would be better. "Better," to them, meant something out there in the future that would come, something that had already started to come. Didn't we ride at the front of the bus? No one stopped to think that one of the reasons we had so little trouble was because we were few in number and seldom left our neighborhood except to shop, work, and get an education.

I began my education at McKinley elementary school where I had excellent teachers who did not tolerate any deviation from their lesson plans. Race was not discussed except in history and geography classes. During recess, however, kids put each other to the time-honored test of brains and brawn. And one of the favorite subjects for this was race. The white kids knew they could get some action if they called one of us a nigger, to which the standard reply was, "If your mother had married who she *really* wanted, you'd be a nigger too." The white kids had heard this reply so many times that we rarely finished the sentence before the fight started. If no white kid started a fight for a few days, we black kids knew all of the magic words that would get a rise out of them, too. My neighborhood also had Swedish Lutherans, Irish Catholics, and Russian Jewish people. By the time I was in the first grade, my vocabulary contained the epithets for all three groups. My common sense told me which members of these groups could be insulted when I was alone and which ones required me to have a backup group. But when the fight was over and it was time to pick a baseball team, the teams were picked on the basis of the players' ability to hit the ball and catch flies.

Aside from these periodic flare-ups, life in elementary school was pretty much the same for everyone. Boys and boys and girls and girls were "best friends," ignoring race. Boys and girls "liked" each other, ignoring race. One day when I was in the fifth grade, and the teacher had left the room, James Nelson said to his red-haired friend, "Jerry, who do you love?" Jerry stood up and said at the top of his voice, "I love Evelyn Edwards." I was so thrilled I ran over to where he was and slapped him as hard as I could.

We children, black and white, slapped each other regu-

Mechanic Arts High School, about 1928

larly, much the same as puppies playing. We sported a few black eyes or scratched faces, but we left no permanent scars.

In 1942 I entered Mechanic Arts High School, where the real differences between races became apparent. Race played a large role in our ability to enjoy the social offerings of the larger community, and it was crucial in our plans for occupations. Although we continued to have white friends in classes, the black kids ate lunch at separate tables and we walked to and from school with other blacks.

Since most of us enjoyed dancing, we had looked forward to attending the "sock hops," the dances given regu-

A crowd at the Harvest Moon Ball watches jitterbugging by black couples, St. Paul Auditorium, 1945.

larly for high school students. The sock hops provided our first major awakening. The white kids did the lindy hop while we did the jitterbug, but both were done to big band music; the only difference was that in the jitterbug, the partners separated and did additional dance steps like the boogie-woogie or the freeze. But because there were more black girls in school than black boys, we really didn't have anyone to dance with. We black girls didn't dance together the way white girls did. Oh, sometimes we'd dance together in the alley when we were learning a new step, but never in public. The white boys didn't ask us to dance, even the ones we had known and played with since kindergarten. They just looked past us as if they didn't know us. After a few times, we stopped going to the school dances, and just went to the dances in our own community.

Most of us were working and when we tried to spend our money for recreation, we found that we were limited there, too. Some of the places, such as Walgreen's drugstore on Seventh and Wabasha, did not openly deny service; they just waited on us last at the lunch counter. We may have only wanted Cokes, but by the time they took our orders, we asked for a full meal. When we saw the waitress bringing the food, we would get up and walk out, leaving the restaurant with a full meal to throw away because someone had told us that the cooks spit in the food when they didn't want to serve you.

Other places, like Bridgeman's soda fountain in downtown St. Paul, flatly refused service. When I was a junior in high school, eight or nine of us started going to Bridgeman's after school and sitting at the counter. The restaurant was very busy at that time of day, and as the waitresses passed us they said, "We don't serve Negroes in here." Our response was, "We know it." We sat there for an hour, not being served and very satisfied that we were affecting their profits for the day. Finally one day the manager called the police. The police told the manager that all of us were acting within our legal rights. The manager could not bar us from the premises since the business was open to the public, but he did have the right to refuse service to us. And since we had the legal right to be there as long as we didn't disturb the peace, there was nothing the police could or would do.

We didn't have the political savvy to notify the press for support. Nor did we have any idea that young blacks throughout the country shared our resentments—and our anger, which would remain unnoticed by most of the white society until the "surprise" riots of the 1960s. So we continued our sit-in, as the technique was later called, until the manager decided it was more profitable to serve us and take a chance on offending the other customers than it was to have us occupy from eight to fifteen stools (we had picked up followers) during the rush hour.

The victory was without reward. By the time we were able to eat the ice cream, we had made enemies of the ones who were serving it. And since we had the old fear of people spitting in our food, we left Bridgeman's for the younger students coming behind us who had not angered the soda jerks.

Being a member of a minority group does not always work against you. For the prom, race worked in our favor. In 1946, for senior girls, the Junior-Senior Prom was the most important event of our lifetime. It was more important than Senior Day, when we taught the classes, or graduation, or getting our first full-time job. It was the evidence that we had succeeded, not only academically, but socially. It was the carrot at the end of the stick that kept us pure. "Bad" girls didn't go to the prom. For most of us, it was the first time we had worn a formal gown, or had gone on a date in a privately owned car (borrowed from an older relative). For the black senior students, it would be the first time that we had entered a major hotel as a guest.

For three years, we had enviously listened to upperclassmen's stories of the prom. When movies containing prom scenes were shown at the Faust Theatre we had sat in the fourth row and watched the gala on the silver screen. The anticipation of being among the select few in our neighborhood who had actually *been* to a prom was almost more than we could stand. Now, this year, at last, it was our time to go.

Prom couples at Mechanic Arts had to be students of the school. When I was a senior there were nine black senior girls—and only four black senior boys. And even though there were a few black junior boys, no self-respecting senior girl would go to the prom with a boy in a lower grade. This was especially true when there was a plot afoot to invite our own dates. And those we wanted to invite were the gallant heroes of our neighborhood returning from the war. All of them having become, through age and experience, MEN.

We understood by now that all rules were subject to exceptions, so we started to work on a plan. We knew that our principal, Mr. James W. Smith, expected thoroughness in everything we did, but we had found him to be a fair man. We assembled our arguments with great care and a will to succeed that would have made our teachers proud.

We included only senior girls in our plan (let the juniors fight their own battles!). Since none of us had been able to afford to attend the prom the year before (adults were always talking about the things they couldn't afford when they were young), we would miss it altogether if we couldn't go this year. And we *would* miss it this year because 1) all of the senior boys already had dates (boys didn't mind taking younger girls); 2) going alone or with another girl was out of the question; 3) we couldn't ask the black male students from other schools, a) because of the Mechanic Arts–students-only regulation and b) even if that were waived, they were already taking girls of their own schools and certainly couldn't afford (we got the phrase "couldn't afford" in again) to go to two proms.

Finally Mr. Smith asked what we had left him no choice but to ask: "Well, what can you do?"

In a flash we had the solution.

"We can invite young men from the neighborhood who are not high school students. There are plenty of them."

As soon as the words were out, Mr. Smith knew we had not stumbled on this solution accidentally, but rather had started with the solution and worked out the problem. But the problem was legitimate and Mr. Smith was a fair man.

He gave us his approval with one condition. The young men we chose must have the approval of our parents and

*James W. Smith, the principal of
Mechanic Arts High School in 1946*

the school (him). That was simple. Like most teenagers, we
had doubts about our parents' ability to judge a fun date,
but both teenagers and parents agreed upon the type of
young man who made an appropriate prom escort. So our
parents approved our choices and Mr. Smith gave his
blessing.

We had learned to use race to our benefit for the first
time, making the Junior-Senior Prom an even more splen-
did event. It was the first time that we had danced all night
at a beautiful downtown hotel ballroom with the handsomest man in the city. That night, for me, Booker T. Ellis
was the handsomest man in St. Paul, if not the world. And
that was the night that the black senior girls of Mechanic
Arts High School took their first tentative steps into the

Evelyn after church with Booker T. Ellis, 1946

world of personal influence and power, glamour and romance.

The prom experience may have made us think that we could move mountains, but we were quickly snatched back to reality when we tried to make career choices. In those days homemaking and mothering were full-time occupations, so the home economics classes, which then emphasized the skills of homemaking rather than decision making, were full of sincere young women learning their trade. The few college-bound students formed a clique that left

Evelyn's graduation picture, 1946

the rest of us out. And those of us who had taken the business courses were either looking over the job market or investigating further business training.

One spring afternoon my third-year accounting class went on a tour of a comptometer school. I was fascinated with this little calculating machine and challenged by the speed and accuracy of the operators. The woman who gave the tour spoke glowingly about the many job opportunities available for people with the skill of comptometer operator backed up with three years of bookkeeping training. After the tour, she asked us to call her individually for an appointment to discuss our "career needs."

As soon as I could I called to make an appointment. Since it was a business call, I used my "white-folk's voice." Although I had been surrounded all of my life by southerners who spoke with southern accents, Mama had forbidden me to reproduce that sound in my own speech. This included the words and phrases that she recognized as being native to her home—words like "gret-n-mine" as in "I've *got a mind* to call her"; "ter-wreck-ler" as in "I'm going downtown *directly*"; "hoe-cake" as in "*Fried bread* is quick to make"; "head" as in "Come here, girl, and let me comb your *hair.*" Responding cheerfully to my "white-folk's voice," the recruiter gave me an appointment for the following day after school.

The next morning, I dressed with great care before leaving for school. I wore one of the dresses that was reserved for church with a new pair of stockings and high-heeled shoes. I made sure that I had a comb and makeup with me so that I could refresh my appearance before the interview. I knew how important it was to make a good impression.

My last class was a study hour, so I left early in order to have plenty of time to walk the few blocks to the school. I arrived early and while I waited, I looked through some of the brochures and business magazines in the waiting room. The pictures in the publications looked so glamorous, especially compared with the dishwashing job that I then held at Montgomery Ward, that I was really excited by the time I was called into the office for the interview.

As we talked about the tuition and length of the course, I noticed that she was becoming more and more uncomfortable. Being black had made me highly sensitive to other people's reactions, and I could trust my instincts to know when someone was uncomfortable. I began to ask questions.

"We graduate on June fourteenth. Is that too late to start the summer session?"

"Well, no. But have you thought of other schools?"

"No, this sounds good to me."

"Frankly, just between you and me and the lamppost, I think the tuition's too high."

"That's not a problem. I'm working."

"We never had a Negro at this school before."

"Does that mean you don't want any?"

"No, no, no, no. It's not that at all." That was one "no" too many. But she continued with them. "No, no, no. It's really not that."

I wasn't going to help her out of it; and besides, I was getting mad. I didn't know at whom or what. But my stomach was tightening up and she was becoming ugly to look at.

I wanted to leave. I got up and started for the door, but my anger turned me around to face her.

"Why didn't you tell me that the school was for white people on the phone?"

"I didn't know you were a Negro on the phone. You didn't sound like one."

"How do Negroes sound on the phone?"

I knew the answer to that but I knew she didn't. So I stood there and waited for her to answer.

"Come and sit down. I'll tell you the reason that we have never had Negroes attending school here."

I came back and sat down, thinking, "This is going to be good."

"We have a placement service here, and we take great pride in the number of students that we place after they finish our course. In fact, I'm the one who goes out and gets the businesses to hire our students. And, frankly, I don't think that I could place you. So you see, it isn't us, but rather the businesses that we have to work with."

She went on talking about what a pity it was that people felt that way. I hated it when white people felt sorry for me. As long as they were mean and belittling, my anger could protect me. But when they became sympathetic, my anger turned to shame and I was left defenseless. If she couldn't get me a job, that meant that there was something wrong with me. That no matter what I did or how well I did it, there was still something wrong with me. She went on and on about the hiring practices of businesses and the way that some people didn't realize that "you people" are human beings too, and the shame spread and spread until it consumed my entire life.

She was totally drained of excuses, but she kept talking anyhow, saying the same things over and over again, with her voice getting higher and higher and her face muscles losing all control. She looked and sounded like a babbling idiot. I got up and left the office.

I walked home from downtown. At some point I took off my shoes. My mind kept asking the same question, "Was there something wrong with me?"

Was there something wrong with me that made people stand up on the streetcar rather than sit next to me? That I couldn't be served in so many restaurants? That little kids would spit at me and call me nigger? I remembered last month when my friend, who was a waitress at Montgomery Ward, had too many people to wait on. I helped her while I was on my lunch break, and then the boss called me in and told me not to do that again, even on my own time, because I was a Negro. Being a Negro meant that there was something wrong with you. All the way home I thought about that. Being a Negro meant that there was something wrong with you. But there hadn't been anything wrong with Mama and Daddy. If the people who made me feel ashamed knew Morris and Oscar they'd know that there was nothing wrong with them. In fact, there wasn't even anything wrong with Aunt Good. She just acted funny, sometimes. Maybe it was just me. Maybe I already knew that there was something wrong with me. Maybe that's why I didn't ever try out for cheerleader, even though everybody in the neighborhood kept telling me to because I could do the cheers better than the cheerleaders at school. I must have known that there was something wrong with me. Yes, there was something wrong with me.

When Morris came home from work, right away he asked me, "What's the matter with you, girl?"

Aunt Good answered, "She's been that way ever since she came in from school. Said she didn't feel like going to work."

"Why didn't you go to work?"

"I didn't feel like it."

"Are you sick? I've never known you to stay home from work."

"There's something wrong with me."

"What do you mean there's something wrong with you? Are you sick?"

Then I told him what had happened at the comptometer school and how I had figured out that there must be something wrong with me. Morris listened. I could tell he was getting mad so I stopped talking, 'cause I didn't want him to be mad at me.

"Girl, there ain't nothing wrong with you. There's something wrong with the world, but there sure ain't nothing wrong with you. You just have to play the game a little different than if you were white. You can do anything any white person can do. You just have to play the game different."

"How can I do anything a white person can do if I can't even get a job, except a job washing dishes?"

"You have to make the man hire you."

"How can I make the man hire me if he doesn't want to?"

"You make the man hire you by being better than anybody else that's applying for the job."

Aunt Good mumbled under her breath, "I've been telling her that for years."

"How can I be better than anybody else? I'm not smarter than anybody else."

"No, you're not smarter than anybody else. But let me tell you how it works. You go to that business school you were talking about and you stay there until you know more than you need to know. If everybody else can get a job adding up twenty columns in an hour, you stay there until you can add up thirty columns in a half hour."

This line of reasoning seemed to prove that there was something wrong with me.

"Why do I have to get overqualified if there's nothing wrong with me?"

"How many times do I have to tell you that there's nothing wrong with you? You should not have to get over-qualified to get a job, but that's the way it is. All of us have to do everything we can do to change the way things are in this world. But meanwhile we have to learn to survive in this world as it is. And to survive, you have to be better in order to be equal. Things will be different by the time you have children. Things are better for you than they were for Mama and they'll be better for your children than they are for you. Meanwhile, get yourself enrolled in that school or some other school. I don't want to hear any more of this foolishness."

Morris was mad now. But it wasn't at me. He went into his bedroom and slammed the door. I heard him curse. Morris didn't curse very often. In a few seconds he came back out and said, "And stop taking time off from work every time something goes wrong in your life. As many things that go wrong in this world, some months you won't work at all."

As usual, Morris had me laughing when he finished and life went on. After all, I couldn't stay down in the dumps too long. There was a dance that night at the Hallie Q. Brown.

I didn't apply at the comptometer school. I just couldn't stand to look at that woman's face again, ever. Instead, I registered at the Globe Business College to study advanced accounting. I remained there as an evening student until I was overqualified for any job I would apply for.

Morris was right. A few years later, I became cashier at Hamline University, their first black staff member, and was written up in our neighborhood newspaper, the *St. Paul Recorder.*

There had been many employment pioneers before us. We joined and multiplied their ranks, and like them we were mindful not to let the door slam shut behind us.

17

Another Perfect Day

When I was nineteen—courtin' age—I worked at the United States Bedding Company in St. Paul operating a power sewing machine. One of my co-workers, who was quite a bit older than I, introduced me to his older brother Bill, who was visiting his family in Minnesota and Wisconsin for an indefinite period of time. Bill was an extremely handsome man with the ease and charm of manner acquired only by extensive travel, both geographically and up and down the social scale. When he asked me to have dinner with him I gladly accepted, and I was flattered when that date led to many others that summer.

Through our many conversations, he told me about his work as a hotel manager in the big cities of the East where there were many black hotels, and he described the different kinds of people from all over the world he had met. He told me about the black entertainers and other artists who traveled between this country and Europe. He knew about foods I had never heard of and the correct wines to have with them. He knew about fashions and books and governments. He brought into my life a world I didn't know existed, and I was fascinated.

My folks were a little disturbed at first because of the twenty-seven-year difference in our ages. But Bill was a polite and honorable man, and soon a calm began to settle on our household about "Evelyn's new fellow." This calm

*Evelyn at age nineteen, standing on
the corner of Kent and Rondo*

turned to sheer panic when I announced one day that Bill
had asked me to marry him, that I had accepted, and that
the following Sunday we were going to Cumberland, Wisconsin, to meet his parents. Aunt Good, Morris, Oscar, and
all other interested parties spent the rest of the week telling
me what life would be like with a man that much older
than I. They progressed year by year.

"When you're only 20, he'll be 47."

"When you're only 21, he'll be 48."

"When you're only 22, he'll be 49."

On and on it went until I was *only* 80 and he was a de-
crepit 107.

Interior of the St. Paul Union Depot, 1949

I either ignored or laughed at this exercise in mathematics.

Early the next Sunday morning Bill came by the house in a cab and we went to the train station. The thrill of entering the St. Paul Union Depot only increased with familiarity. And I was very familiar with it—the yearly trips with Mama, and later the monthly train trips to Minneapolis with my teenage friends, the visits to the station to pick up people coming in, and the many, many times my friends and I went there just to hang out. As with everything else we did we were under constant supervision, because if we weren't related to one of the redcaps, they were friends of at least one of our families.

That Sunday morning was one of those summer days that attaches us forever to this state. The sun was not really shining, it was just there to light up the day so we could see how beautiful it was. It brought warmth, not just to feel,

but the color of warmth. There was a breeze that moved the
leaves a little, and the smell that let us know that fall was
near. Maybe it was the smell of the ripe apples or maybe
leaves smell different just before they turn to their autumn
colors. But it wasn't fall, it was still summer and the sweater
that felt good early in the morning would soon be taken off
and stored until evening. The train ride to Cumberland was
exactly what could be expected. The train seat reminded
me of my Mama-made nest in the back rows of the Sanctified church, and Bill's conversation, never far from humor, matched the day exactly.

The train left the harvested farmlands on the plains of
Minnesota and entered the rolling hills of Wisconsin. It
went around lakes, over rivers, and through forests. Looking out of the window was like flipping through thousands
of picture postcards. Each second the scene was different
and sometimes it included people waving to us from their
spot in the picture.

It was a short ride, and when we reached Cumberland
there was one taxi sitting outside the depot. That was all
that was necessary because we were the only people who got
off the train.

The driver was leaning against his cab. When Bill asked
him if he knew where the Johnson farm was he looked first
at Bill, and then at me, nodded his head as he said "Yeah,"
but didn't move.

"Good. We'd like to go there."

The driver still didn't move, just looked back and forth
between Bill and me. Bill took a deep breath and, with a
look of extreme boredom, said, "They're my parents." The
driver looked hard at Bill again, thought a question that he
didn't ask, and opened the door for us to get in.

Bill had already told me how often he had gone
through this scene. He and his two brothers were the children of an interracial marriage. When his father, who was
black, died, his mother had remarried a white farmer who

had been independent enough of spirit and purse to ignore the criticism of his neighbors. Besides being a good provider and a gentle husband for their mother, Mr. Johnson was a caring father to the three boys. Bill had been looking forward to this trip.

As the cab neared the farm, Bill began to relax. And by the time we drove into the yard, the smile that he had used to tell me about the farm had returned.

His mother and stepfather were waiting in the yard when we got there, and they pushed each other out of the way reaching in the cab for him. The driver had to wait until we got out, both parents hugged him, and I was introduced as "the girl I told you about in my letter," before he was paid. His hat came off in respect when he saw the size of the tip, and, with the sincerity of a longtime friend, he assured us he would return to pick us up in time to take the evening train back to St. Paul.

I had never been in a farmhouse before. I had expected it to be like Aunt Good's house in Macon. In some ways, it was — it wasn't very fancy, but everything about it seemed useful. There were tools hanging on large nails and hooks on the outside. There was a mud scraper on the step entering the back door and the house hadn't had a coat of paint since the barn had. The small house was clean inside, but not polished, and its large kitchen held all the furniture except the beds.

We had coffee and homemade rolls while the Johnsons listened to their oldest son's tales and adventures. Neither of them had traveled much, so they were interested in every aspect of every city he had traveled to since they had last seen him.

Then it was their turn to bring him up to date about life on the farm. They had stopped farming a few years ago and now only kept a small garden for their own food and "to give Daddy something to do." After about an hour or so, the thirst for news was quenched and Bill said, "I think I'll show Evelyn the place now. We'll be back in a bit."

"Take your time. We have to get dinner on anyway."

The farm was probably not so very large, but it was more land owned by one person than I had ever seen. It was in rolling country, with a good-sized pond just over one of the small hills. We sat down by the water without talking, just enjoying being there. After a while, he started telling me about his memories of this farm, his chores, his goat, his brothers, and the deep love and respect he held for this man who had married his mother.

The smell of the food cooking rode by on the wind and we headed back to the house. The Johnsons had changed to their Sunday clothes, which were really only clean sets of the clothes they had been wearing. But you could tell that they had dressed for a special occasion. The special occasion was not our visit, but their regular Sunday service. And they were very pleased that their congregation had doubled this Sunday.

Three of the kitchen chairs were sitting side by side in the middle of the room, and the fourth was sitting before them. Mrs. Johnson, Bill, and I sat facing Mr. Johnson, and church service began when Mr. Johnson stood and said, "Let us pray."

He gave a short, stiff prayer of thanksgiving and then sat down as Mrs. Johnson thumbed through the hymnal until she found the song she wanted to sing. She held the book out in front of her so we could see it too, nodded her head to each of us, and then we started to sing with her. When we had sung all four verses and one extra chorus, she closed the book. Mr. Johnson stood up with his Bible in his hand, read the chapter from the Book of Job in which the devil dares God to test Job by removing his blessings from him, closed his Bible, and gave a sermon on that text. Mr. Johnson was certainly not an orator, not in the traditions I had heard throughout my life. But he did have a common-

sense approach to the text and a friendly manner of speaking that held my attention and gave me something to think
about. After he finished the sermon, it was testimony time.
His wife started out. Her testimony was a simple statement
of thanks for bringing her son once more to her door and
a request for his safekeeping until he returned to her. She
then looked at Bill, who stood up and gave the same testimony in reverse. And when he sat down, I knew it was my
turn. I stood up and said how glad I was to share this day
with them. This seemed to be all right because Mr. Johnson
stood up again and gave a closing prayer.

The atmosphere changed as soon as the prayer was over.
The chairs were put back around the big kitchen table. Mrs.
Johnson put a clean apron on over the clean housedress,
and she and her husband started to set the table. I asked
if I could help and was told, "No, of course not. You're a
guest. Bill, why don't you show her where to wash up." So
I washed up in a washbasin in the back hall and we all sat
down to eat.

At my house the meals were a kind of celebration. They
were long and noisy with several compliments to the cook
and a joke or two about the dishwasher. At Bill's parents'
house the meal was quiet and deliberate, as simple as the
food we were eating. The meal was soon over and our offer
to help with the dishes received another firm no.

Mrs. Johnson took a pitcher of fresh lemonade from the
icebox and we all went outside to the picnic table with Mr.
Johnson carrying the glasses. This time the conversation was
more relaxed and they asked about my family and what
kind of work I did, and the afternoon passed.

Soon, the cab driver was back to pick us up. It took a
while to say good-bye, because the Johnsons had no idea
when they would see their son again. It came out in the
day's conversation that he always sent them money, but he
just didn't get home very often. And so they delayed him

a little longer than necessary, and because he loved them, he let them.

The cab driver was talkative on the trip to the station, telling us what fine folks the Johnsons were, and what a good farmer Mr. Johnson had been, and what fine Christians they were, and, oh yes, come to think about it, he had heard about the sons they had.

The train ride home was quiet. The picture postcards dimmed and then were gone into the dark before we reached St. Paul. Bill and I sat close together but we were far apart in our thoughts. I'm sure Bill was thinking about the past, while my mind played with the future.

At precisely the right moment, the train slowed, the whistle blew, and people started to move and talk softly to each other. The porters and the conductor were collecting the things to be collected and I slid my hand under Bill's and said, "This has been the most perfect day of my life."

A little while after that, the summer was gone and so was Bill. I'm not sure what happened. We were friendly until the end and then we were sad. I think Bill needed a companion instead of a student and I know I needed a dance partner more than a teacher.

But no matter what happened, it couldn't erase that perfect day.

18

Ten Years Later

The next ten years brought abrupt, drastic changes to my family. I moved to Milwaukee after Aunt Good died, then homesickness drove me back to St. Paul after only fourteen months. Oscar moved up to Oatmeal Hill, and when I was twenty-nine, Morris killed a man.

He pleaded not guilty to first-degree murder. But the jury thought otherwise and sentenced him to life imprisonment in the Minnesota State Prison at Stillwater.

Someone told me the details, but I didn't hear them. All I knew was that Morris was gone forever, for in those days when the accused was found guilty of murder in the first degree and the sentence was life imprisonment, that's exactly how much time he served.

I was again in business college at the time, this time studying legal stenography. When I finished, I went to the St. Paul Urban League to see what openings were available for an experienced clerical worker with additional training. The director at that time was Whitney M. Young, Jr., a hardworking man dedicated to the goals of the league, especially in the workplace. He later became the president of the National Urban League, continuing this work until his tragic death by drowning during a visit to Nigeria in 1971.

The Urban League was housed in three small rooms in a downtown office building. The secretary was out of the office when I arrived, and Mr. Young himself took my ap-

Whitney M. Young, Jr., head of the National Urban League in the 1960s

plication. He read through my history of work and education and said, "Come on in my office. This shouldn't be too hard; after all, you're certainly qualified for the work you're asking for."

He opened a file drawer, lifted out a folder, and placed it in front of him on the desk. As he searched through it, he told me jokingly that there was an opening at Stillwater State Prison for a Clerk Steno II.

Much to his surprise, I said, "I'd like that one."

"You don't have to take the first one that I mentioned. There's other jobs here."

"No, I want that one."

Even though I wanted the job, I immediately recognized three problems. First, I had to pass the state exam. Second, Stillwater was twenty-two miles east of St. Paul and I didn't own or drive a car. The third problem I chose not to think about right then.

The state exam was easy, because I was trained to take shorthand at 120 words per minute and the exam required only 80. After I passed, the clerk showed me several state jobs within the city that were open to a person of my qualifications. But my mind was set on working at the prison. I made an appointment to interview the following week. Then came the second problem — transportation. I took the city bus up to Stillwater and then transferred to the Bayport bus, which took me to the prison. One trip told me that I had to make other arrangements.

After the prison's personnel director had taken my application and interviewed me, he told me that he found me acceptable, but the final decision was the warden's.

Douglas Rigg had been the warden at San Quentin before he moved to Minnesota. My first impression of him fit the movie stereotype of wardens at San Quentin. That impression wasn't lessened by his office arrangement. The room was about sixteen feet square, but it seemed to be four times that size. In front of a large window at one end of the room sat a mammoth, dark-stained oak desk. Warden Rigg occupied a swivel captain's chair behind it. Near the other end of the room were five or six large upholstered chairs, the nearest one being at least half a room away from the warden's desk.

He motioned me to a chair (not the nearest one), read

my application, and then started telling me about the prison, from time to time asking a pointed question. He acted as if he had all the time in the world, and as he talked, I became more comfortable. When he finally said the magic words, "When can you start?" I knew that it was the moment to deal with the third problem.

"There's something I think I should tell you before I start. It may affect whether or not I can work here."

By now he was sitting forward in his chair. But when I said that, he leaned back, enlarging the space between us, and gave me the look of a person who has heard a million stories and is really not in the mood to hear one more. His silence said, "What is it?"

"My brother is in prison here."

"What's your brother's name?"

"Morris."

"Morris what?"

"Keaton."

"First-degree murder." It wasn't a question, but I answered anyhow.

"Yes."

"How do you feel about your brother being here?"

"Sad."

"He pleaded not guilty. Do you think he was guilty?"

"I don't know."

He was quiet for awhile and I wondered why I thought I could get a job here. I knew that the families of prisoners were just as much social outcasts as the prisoners themselves. I could sense that the people already working in the offices didn't even know a prisoner, much less have one for a relative. But Morris wasn't a prisoner, he was my brother.

Finally Warden Rigg leaned forward again and said, "You didn't answer my question. When can you start?"

"Tomorrow."

He smiled for the first time and shook his head. "I'm

afraid that's too early for you. You still have to solve your transportation problem. How about next week?"

He got up from his desk and came around it to meet me as I got up. He held his hand out, and as he held mine he said, "Unfortunately, you won't be able to talk with your brother. And the staff doesn't need to know that you're related to one of our inmates. They're a pretty pious bunch and may give you some trouble. Good luck."

I left the prison very happy. When I got back to St. Paul I bought a car on credit and started to learn to drive. I called Edgar Pillow, who was a probation officer at the prison, and told him that I would be starting there the following week. I had known Ed most of my life. He was a few years older than I, so I didn't associate with him much, but I knew him from church and social activities in the community. His family lived on Oatmeal Hill and he was one of the few blacks who went to college after high school.

Ed was so glad to hear there would be another black at the prison that when I told him that I didn't know how to drive, he offered to park his car at my house in the mornings and let me drive my car to Stillwater until I could pass my driver's exam. Ed had a lot of guts. Of course, he knew that I was Morris's sister and it just so happened that he was Morris's probation officer, which gave me knowledge of how things were going for Morris.

The prison is divided into two sections, in front of the gate—the area of the prison that can be reached from the street through unlocked doors—and behind the gate. I worked with several inmates in front of the gate in the business office, but Morris was stationed behind the gate, in the main dining room. I went behind the gate regularly, to the employee dining room and to the treatment and custody offices. This allowed me to see him from time to time. We would hold silent conversations and hug each other from across the room.

I had one other means of contact with Morris while I was

there. One of my duties was to work in the censor's office, and I had access to his mail. I found out that his spirits were high and that he hoped some day to earn a parole, although very few people convicted of first-degree murder ever had. But I also felt saddened and angry as I watched his girlfriend slip away from him and other friends stop writing altogether. And I noticed that Oscar wasn't writing. I also felt ashamed about the few times I had written. I knew that Morris had a strong will, but could he withstand the abandonment as well as the life sentence? I couldn't do anything at all about it. Anything that was read in the censor's office had to be held in the strictest confidence. It was made clear to me that I would be fired on the spot if I discussed anything I had read with anyone.

There were only two exceptions to this rule. If a close relative of an inmate died, that letter was routed to the man's parole officer, the social worker, or the chaplain. Or if there was an indication that the inmate might be planning to leave the institution without the blessing of the state, the letter was routed to the custody office. The censor's office foiled many prison breaks.

Since Morris was not buckling under the pressure of loneliness, he was not a security risk, so I couldn't discuss it with the staff. Also, I couldn't talk to his girlfriend about it because she might report me for breaking the confidentiality rule. So I suffered silently for and with Morris for the year and a half I worked at the prison.

Just before I left my job, I sent a kite — an interoffice memo — to Warden Rigg, asking for permission to visit with Morris on my last day of employment. He granted my request and in turn sent a kite to Morris asking if he wanted to see me. I lived in suspense while Morris took two days to think about it. He knew that if it became known that I had a brother in prison, it would affect my chances of returning to state employment. Since he knew that I had thought about that before I had made the request, he went against his better judgment and granted the visit.

On my last day of work, I dressed in my good black dress, paying special attention to my makeup and hair so that I would look as good as I could—not for the fancy dinner party that my co-workers were taking me to after work, but for my morning appointment with my brother. More than ever before I wanted him to be proud of me, because I knew how fast all information passed through the prison population.

I got to the visiting room first. The room was smaller than I thought it would be. The guard's desk and chair were elevated on a platform at one end, and the remaining space was taken up with two double-length tables the width of a picnic table. In the center of the tables was a partition about twelve inches high. The guard was close enough to hear the general idea of the conversation (whispering was not allowed) and high enough to see all contact between the inmate and the visitor.

When Morris came in, I reached for him immediately. With the table between us, we hugged and kissed and cried. At least I hugged and kissed and cried. Morris kept patting my back and saying, "It's all right, Ba'. Everything's all right, Ba'. Now stop crying, Ba'." And pretty soon I did and we talked and sometimes held hands over the partition until our time was up. And then I left. I believed him when he said he was going to walk out the door a free man. I knew if anybody could, Morris would.

19

Epilogue

In his sixth year at Stillwater, Morris was transferred to minimum security. He became Warden Rigg's chauffeur, and he moved from behind the gate to the farm colony. Our visits became much more pleasant because we could talk privately in the visitors' living room, and he told me about life in prison. Some of the stories were scary, some sad. And since Morris's sense of humor was still intact, some were very funny.

At the end of nine years, Morris walked out of the state prison on a lifetime parole; five years later his life-style and his vocational progress had convinced the parole board he was no longer a threat to society, so he was released from parole. He worked at construction jobs until 1969, when he was hired by the Minnesota Division of Vocational Rehabilitation (DVR) as a counselor's aide. In that same year I began work for DVR as a counselor, and our offices were side by side at Pilot Center in Minneapolis.

It was like the old days being with Morris again, except he had become wiser and calmer. He used the same intelligence, patience, and determination to climb the career ladder with DVR as he had to free himself from prison. When he retired from state employment in 1983 he was working as an aide to the assistant commissioner of economic security, a position that brought him frequently in contact with

the governor of Minnesota. After his retirement he returned to Macon.

Oscar worked as a Pullman porter on the Soo Line railroad until his retirement in 1980. There was no argument
between us, but from the time I moved to Minneapolis, in
1960, we saw little of each other; like Aunt Good, he was
a very private person. In 1987 he lost a leg to diabetes and,
rather than going to a nursing home, he moved to Macon,
where Morris took care of him. During this time, the two
boys and I were very close. He died in October 1987.

I don't want to leave readers with the impression that
I have been sitting on the sidelines, observing, all my life.
My basic curiosity and a few government loans earned me
a bachelor's degree and took me halfway through a master's
program at the University of Minnesota, after which I
worked in the field of human services. My marriages were
not successful, but they ended with good will. My children,
Luana Lynette, Aaron Joseph, and Robert Edward, have
been a constant joy to me (except on the days when they
weren't); my granddaughters, Jessica Lyn and Heather Ash-
ley, keep my life fresh. In 1978 I bought a small tree farm
in central Minnesota, and in 1980 I was seriously injured in
an automobile accident as I drove to it. Four years later,
when I finally backed away from that pain, I went to work
for Augsburg Fortress, Publishers, and became the opera-
tions supervisor in the data processing department.

The community that I wrote about is gone. It was erased
by the highway department and "progress"—other people's money. U.S. Interstate 94 was built through the old
Rondo neighborhood in the 1960s. From 1970 to 1989,
when it closed, the Faust Theatre showed movies unsuit-
able for children. The neighborhood storefronts on Dale
and Selby, where I paid ten cents for paper dolls, suffered
and closed when the corner became a high-crime area, then
began a process of renovation. The Hallie moved to a new

Construction of Interstate Highway 94 at Dale Street and St. Anthony Avenue, about 1966

location on Kent and Iglehart and became the Martin Luther King Center, where children learn about Dr. King the same way we learned about Hallie Q. Brown.

There is busing now, so kids don't necessarily go to the same school as their neighbors, forming lifetime bonds. The black population has grown so large that we don't all know each other. We weren't the first generation of blacks born in Minnesota, but we think of ourselves as FF's (First Families) now. The hunger for the old days is so great that in 1983 a group of St. Paul people started an annual celebration called Rondo Days in an effort to remember and re-create at least the atmosphere of our community. I share that hunger. It makes me write stories.